THE TRADESMAN'S
SURVIVAL
GUIDE

THE ULTIMATE GUIDE
TO TAKE YOU FROM
BUSY TRADESMAN TO
SUCCESSFUL
BUSINESS OWNER

JOE DOYLE.

This 1st Edition Was September Published 2021

Address:
Unit D4A,
Station Road Business Park,
Clondalkin Industrial Estate,
Dublin 22.

Website:
www.joedoyle.ie

Typeset by Karl Hempton

ISBN: 978-1-913108-58-8

Printed and Bound by eprint books limited, Dublin, Ireland.
35, Coolmine Industrial Estate, Blanchardstown, Dublin 15.

A special thank you to Linda who
I can never thank enough.

Table Of Contents

To access any Downloads mentioned in this book go to:
www.joedoyle.ie/tsgfreeresources

To access any Downloads mentioned in this book go to:
www.joedoyle.ie/tsgfreeresources

Preface

Before you start reading this book you need to know that all of the content is not exclusively owned by me or designed by me. What I am writing in this book is a combination of everything I have learned in all my business dealings and negotiations to date, it is what I have learned as a result of spending countless hours and tens of thousands of euros on my own personal growth and development, from reading dozens of books and blog posts and online articles.

It is what I have learned from my company carrying out works in over 2,500 private individual homes all over the country. It is what I have learned from being involved in over 100 property deals. It is what I have learned from being ripped off along the way, from being sued along the way, from being threatened and intimidated and, most importantly, it is what I have learned from my own foolish mistakes along the way.

I am predicting right now that many people will read this book and learn a lot from it, a percentage of people will try to implement their version of the tools described in the book and they will reach out to me to explain why something didn't work. We will look under the hood for them to see that they didn't follow the processes exactly as described and we will be able to see where the mistake occurred. If you are going out to implement these processes into your business, try to stick exactly to the format as much as possible as they have been carefully crafted over many years.

I want to thank all of the lads from the 52 STEPS TO A BETTER BUSINESS group, without you this book would not have been possible; you say you have learned a lot from me, well I have learned just as much from you guys. I have mentioned a few lads throughout the book to give examples of the changes and improvements you have gotten in your business so fair play to all.

I also want to say thank you to the guys within the 52 STEPS community who have made the effort to help other lads in the community who haven't yet made as much progress on their journey as you have on yours.

Remember at all times -

Trial and error is out, we need to learn from the mistakes of others.

Introduction

This book is not about me or my life story so far, it's purely about helping you get your shit together to improve your business and help you make more money. Each chapter will have lessons in it that you can start to apply to your business today so flick straight to chapter 1 to get cracking or, if you would like to find out a little bit about myself and who I am, then it may be worthwhile to invest a few minutes of your time to read the next few pages of this introduction...

My name is Joe Doyle and I want to start off by saying thanks for buying or illegally downloading my book. What would piss me off more than you illegally downloading my book would be you buying it and not utilising the knowledge that's inside it. So, whether you bought, borrowed or stole this book please go and put it to good use.

When I'm out and about people stop me and say you're Joe from Facebook, you're Joe the landlord, you're Joe the property fella, you're Joe the millionaire fella from Facebook. People put all sorts of titles on me and I'm cool with that, at least they know me, that's the main thing, but now I'm gonna give you my version of who I am.

My name is Joe Doyle and in addition to being a father, a son, a brother, a friend, a non meat-eater (I don't like the term vegan), a part-time endurance runner, an employer, a former bricklayer turned property investor. I am also Ireland's top business mentor for tradesmen and the construction industry. And now that this book is out, I suppose I'm an author as well.

I'm very fortunate that I currently have a number of successful businesses and life for me is good financially. But it wasn't always this smooth and I'm gonna share some of my story so far with you.

I'm most definitely not someone who you would expect to write a book as my spoken English is terrible, I don't think I'd be getting a job at the BBC anytime soon. And as one lad wrote on one of my Facebook videos one day: 'Is this chap for real, he sounds more like he would be robbing your house rather than buying it off you!!!'

For this intro, I'll be writing it exactly as if I was having a conversation with you face to face. I might even leave the typos in for this part; after all, I'm not the chap that wrote Game of Thrones, George RRR Martin, after all, I'm Joe a former bricklayer from Clondalkin. My goal for the intro part of the book is to allow you to get to know me a bit.

I grew up in an estate called Quarryvale in Clondalkin and when I left school I started working with me Da (I was nearly gonna write Dad there wtf). He ran a small building company doing extensions and renovations all around Clondalkin & Ballyfermot and that general area. I left school just after the junior cert and I always knew I was gonna become a bricklayer and serve my time with the aul lad. He had about 5 or 6 lads working for him and my two mates started working with him as well. I needed to wait til I was 16 before I could officially start my apprenticeship, so I was tipping away working with him doing all bits of labouring. I got a seriously good foundation as to how a business operates from these short few years. I needed to look at how me Da ran his business and then do it the opposite.

His business was completely chaotic, full of ups and downs and arguments with different people, both staff and customers. It was an absolutely crazy time and myself and my two mates really enjoyed it, but there was definitely a lot of shenanigans going on in the business that I remember on plenty of occasions asking myself if that is really how things were supposed to be done.

I have one moment that sticks in my head as a complete light bulb moment when I figured that the way he ran his business was not the best way of operating.

There was a rule when building extensions for customers and that was that workers were not allowed in the house. The entire extension would be built and the breakout into the house was the last thing to be done. Normally it was a 40 sqm extension on the back of a house that had a sliding door from the kitchen into the back garden. A fair enough and practical approach to take.

Continually throughout the job, I would hear various tradesmen asking for the plans to check a measurement or something.

Where's he gone with the plans, tell him to come back with them right away. It was a constant chase up of whoever decided to leave the site with the drawings in their pocket without realising.

So, one day I came up with an idea. If the sliding door was going to be the last thing to come out. Why don't I stick the drawings to the glass of the sliding door? But sure they'll get soaked in the rain. But if I stick them to the inside of the door they will be grand, it just means I'd need to break the rules and go inside the house.

Anyways the next day I sneaked into the house and stuck the drawings on to the inside of the patio door with the details facing outwards into the back garden where we were working. It was handy then that everyone knew where the drawings were for the rest of the job. But the real lightbulb moment came when one of the other workers on the site looked at the drawing and laughed. I thought he was laughing cos I had used my head but that wasn't it.

He said look, some head case is after being stuck for a bit of paper to hold down the brickie's line and they ripped off a piece of the drawing. It doesn't take a genius to know that apart from the cheque you get for payment of the job, the second most important piece of paper is the plans for the job. From that day onwards I was always second-guessing if the way the business was being run was the way the business should actually be run.

A while later when I first started my own business I remember complaining to my accountant that there was way more paperwork involved in running my business than I ever seen in my Da's and although he didn't know my Da, he said to me that if I wanted to do it right I would have to do it the way he was telling me to run it.

It wasn't long later before the aul lad started to scale back works and then he got into a load of hassle with the revenue for not paying his taxes correctly. Normally, that alone would be enough to prompt a man to get his act together but not my aul lad, he's a different breed altogether. Eventually, it got to the point where they locked him up for a few weeks until he eventually paid off what he owed and got his act together.

It wasn't long after his escapade with the revenue that I was selected for audit 'randomly' the second time. The first time a few years previous it was an audit for RCT, this time they wanted to audit my entire company and also me personally. Very stressful time and very distracting from the running of the business but we got through it in the end and managed to resume operations.

So, it was my time working with the aul lad and seeing how he ran his things that made me realise I wanted to do things 100% by the book and keep it very professional. I also decided that one day I was gonna become a hot shot property investor and I had started saving for my first house when I was 15 years old. My plan was to buy a house on my 18th birthday. I stuck the head down and kept focused and when I was about 17 years old, my next-door neighbour who lived alone, unfortunately, died so my Da decided he would buy the house. It took ages for the sale to go through and by the time it did go through I was old enough to get a mortgage and I was now on the property ladder.

I had no hesitation in knowing what I wanted to do as a career choice, I was going to be a builder/property guy and I was gonna buy land and build houses to rent them out. Simples. How much more difficult can it be, little did I know I was only a few years away from a massive property crash and recession by which time I would be €3million in debt to the banks. But that's a conversation for later.

By the time I was about 19 years old and just about to finish my apprenticeship I had enough exposure to seeing a business not being run correctly and as such I was now 100% focused on becoming a proper professional businessman and that was that.

Outside of the business end of things, I was living in Clondalkin, we jokingly called the estate the hood. At times it was fairly rough up there and you didn't have to go very far to find trouble. From the time myself and all my mates were in our early teens we just hung around the estate mostly at the shops and we were all just a general nuisance in the area. Pretty much any unsavoury behaviour you can think of going on went on. Myself and my mates were all becoming products of our environment and some more so than others.

It wasn't long before some lads began to get into trouble with the Garda which was a path that led a few of them to prison, some got hooked on drugs and unfortunately a couple died which became a consequence of the path their life was on. For myself, while I was only more than happy to hang around the corners as a teenager drinking and being a nuisance to the community, thankfully I realised before it was too late that this is not the life I wanted to live. But there was one event that completely gave me the absolute inspiration to keep myself 100% on the straight and narrow and not be hanging around street corners.

Down through the years, I regularly got my friends work with my Da. There were 2 of my good friends who worked with him for a good few years before they broke away. One of them was in the process of becoming a carpenter and the other a bricklayer when they finished working with him.

My friend who was in the process of becoming a carpenter unfortunately allowed himself to develop a drug addiction. I remember the day we were at a house party and he took out a bottle of green liquid and suggested we all try it. He said he took some the other day and it was a great buzz. I said no way fuck that and I left the house, but I didn't leave purely because he took out this green liquid, I wasn't bothered by it. It just didn't interest me at all. If you want to go and take this shit work away it's none of my business but it's not for me. That was the attitude of most of us at the time, we had become desensitised to anything any normal person would scream cop the fuck on.

To access any Downloads mentioned in this book go to:
www.joedoyle.ie/tsgfreeresources

Anyways, I left the party and went to another party in the next estate over and on my way home I walked back past the first house. I could see the lights on, so I walked up to the door and went into the house.

There were a few lads still there, there was sick all over the place, one of the lads had puked on himself in his sleep. The place was like a scene out of Trainspotting. I just thought to myself thank fuck I didn't go near that shit. Over the course of the next year or so my friend who was training to become a carpenter developed a serious addiction and he was too proud to admit it to anyone. One night things got too much for him and he took his own life, he left a young child behind him just a few months old.

This had a big effect on me personally as he was one of my best friends. Of the wide group of friends that I had, there were 3 who I was closest to. I didn't know how to deal with this stuff, but I knew it was a series of unfortunate decisions that led to this outcome.

My other friend who I mentioned was in the process of becoming a bricklayer started to miss days at work. He was living in my parents' house at the time and he got on really well with my Da. But he started missing days at work, not coming home for days at a time and he began hanging around with a new group of people. Eventually, he moved out of the house and gave up working with my Da. It wasn't long before some of the decisions started to impact his life. He got into trouble with the Garda and got locked up.

3 weeks after my first friend died, I got a call from someone who rang me up to ask if I was doing ok as he had heard my friend had died. I told him I was holding up ok, but he had things wrong as it was my carpenter friend who had died not my bricklayer friend. He assured me that he had just got a call from someone he knew in 'The Joy' to say my friend had died. I knew he was telling the truth but how in the name of god could two people in their early twenties just die in different circumstances, it just didn't seem real, unfortunately, it was.

I remember I was sitting on a junction box in a house where we were working eating a roll with chicken and cheese on it. I went completely numb. Only one person had told me the news but my phone was hopping so deep down I knew it must be true. Rather than answer the calls and confirm what had happened, I actually just knocked my phone off. I point blank refused to accept that this had happened and I continued working for about an hour. I wasn't ready to deal with this shit. After a few hours I had to turn the phone back on and face the reality. It took a long time for me to get over that and I wasn't right in the head for a good while.

When I eventually did come out of that dark place it was very weird for me because after my first friend took his own life I thought it was the worst thing someone could ever have to deal with, but then to have to deal with another death less than a month later it showed me that no matter how bad things are they can always get worse.

To access any Downloads mentioned in this book go to:
www.joedoyle.ie/tsgfreeresources

Thankfully since then, I have never had to deal with such a sudden double tragedy but when things go wrong in business for me I think back on those days and tell myself if I can get through that I can get through anything

I'm sure you have heard the fable of the twin brothers who were the sons of an alcoholic. One of the twins never drank a day in his life and the other twin also became an alcoholic just like the father.

When the twins were both individually asked about how they came to be the person they are, they both had the same answer:

Look at my father, how else would you expect me to turn out.

Well, that was me, I had seen how someone's life can be messed up if they don't attempt to control their environment and commit to going along a certain path in life.

Growing up in the land of opportunity

In the previous few pages, I have given you the personal side of what's shaped me into being the person I am today. I'm sure those few pages could be turned into a number of chapters or maybe even a book itself. But you will also notice I didn't name anyone other than my Da and I was vague enough with some details.

The reason for this is, this book is about business and its not another X-Factor style sob story, and I don't want to run the risk of upsetting any of the lads' families, but most importantly these two guys were my best friends, we classed ourselves as brothers and if I'm going to introduce you to them I won't be just introducing them as a fact or a statistic I will need to allow you the opportunity to get to know them.

You need to hear all the stories and antics that we got up to, all the scrapes and escapades that happened. All the absolute mad carry on that happened and all the times we got into trouble. If you do want an image of the two lads think Conor & Jock from the young offenders, just as likeable but a shade less innocent, with a few streaks of the villain from the show Billy Murphy intertwined in each of them.

To access any Downloads mentioned in this book go to:
www.joedoyle.ie/tsgfreeresources

At the same time this book is not specifically about me, it's about helping you as a tradesman and business owner make more money.

In the same way that I became inspired to become a top-class businessman by how my aul lad ran his business.

And in the same way that I became inspired to make good decisions by the bad decisions my two best friends made that ultimately led to their deaths.

I then began to seek inspiration in the community around me. I took a matter of fact stock take of myself and my situation. I came to the conclusion that I was growing up in the land of opportunity. Now bear in mind I was growing up in a crime-ridden, drug-ridden, anti-social behaviour ridden (to put it mildly) estate, suicide was an all too frequent event plus there were some people who had been murdered in the area.

But for now, I was gonna set that aside. I was going to change my perspective. I did the numbers on the entire situation as they call it, and I came to the conclusion that I was growing up in the land of opportunity and here's why:

A lot of people were full time unemployed and many by their own choice. Of those who were employed, none of those jobs stuck out to me as anything other than an average job. Lots of people's homes were owned by the council. People in the community were being prosecuted and sent to prison on the regular for all sorts of crimes and nobody seemed to care. Most people didn't go to college. It seemed to me that most people were not trying and failing, but they were actually setting the bar very, very low and then succeeding at it. Now I'm not saying nobody in Clondalkin has a good job or nobody goes to college and all that jazz.

What I am saying is that I noticed in my community and in my circle of people this was the norm. If this was the norm for my social circle it meant that if I failed in business there would be no fall from grace. Nobody would even bat an eyelid.

I was blessed that in order to simply blend in, I didn't need to get a college degree. I didn't need to get a €500k mortgage and I didn't need €50k worth of cars in the garden. When I came up with this evaluation, I began to feel some pity for those poor unfortunate souls who grew up in those affluent areas.

I was born at the right time and in the exact perfect location. I was born into the land of opportunity and with all that in mind...

Shall we begin ... ...

Chapter 1

What is the purpose of your business?

Here's a question for you.

What is the purpose of your business?

I have asked that question to people who have been in business for many years and I see a blank stare on their face after which they then say – To make money.

Really the response they give of 'To make money' is just a reply they spout off as they most likely have never thought about this before.

This book is called The Tradesman's Survival Guide for that exact reason, to help tradesmen survive and to have a reference point to look back on in the event of something going wrong for them in their business.

But what you need to understand and accept as truth is the fact that most businesses regardless of their size, be it a micro- enterprise like yours, or be it a massive big company.

Most of them do not stand the test of time, for one reason or another they change, shut down, or are bought out by other companies.

Whilst my expertise covers small businesses in the construction sector so I can't comment from experience on other industries I can tell you that the reason most businesses like yours don't do well over time is that the owner has not set out a clearly defined purpose for the business.

Business owners say – well the purpose of my business is to make money. I then ask how much; they reply as much as possible. Do you have a figure in mind and the next reply is usually XXX amount per year?

Depending on the individual who I am asking these questions of at the time will usually determine how much X always means to them but it's generally the same reply.

This to me shows a major lack of focus and a major lack of clarity because once you get this part of your business correct, you will realise that everything that you do in your business is done purely to allow your business to achieve its purpose. The more you are willing to stick to the purpose of the business, the more you are likely to become successful and achieve that purpose.

Just think of the last time you got into your car and drove to someplace. The purpose of you getting into your car and driving off was not to get into your car and get somewhere random nor was it to get there at a random time. You had a very defined purpose and that's the reason you got into your car. You wanted to be in a certain location at a very specific time. By having this location and time in mind before even starting the journey you knew what was required of you to get there.

So, let's flick back to your business, saying the purpose of your business is to simply make money is the same as saying that the purpose of the car is just to drive you to someplace. It lacks decisiveness and it lacks accuracy.

As you read this you will probably scratch your head a little bit and probably start to come up with a purpose for your business but let me help you out here.

If you are running a business with up to 5 employees including yourself, I want you to take on the following as the purpose of your business:

The purpose of your business is to provide you with a clear profit of €500 per day so that you can take care of your family financially.

Now it's not any of my business to give you the purpose for your own business, that's something you will need to do yourself later. But roll with me on this and for now, adopt this as the purpose for your business. Usually, when I unveil to someone the temporary purpose for their business, I get one of two responses. The first being – There's no way I can ever make that kind of money, not in my line of work or not in my area. My reply to them is – Not with that attitude, you won't make it that's for sure. The second most common response I get is, sure if I only made €500 per day, I would be losing money. I would be going out of business sure I make far more than that as it is.

We can then check this by applying a little test which is quite simple.

If you make €500 clear profit per day or 20 days that's €10,000. If you make €500 per day and you have been making it for the last 12 months you should have €120,000 in your bank. Many people believe on the face of it that they are making it but when we look under the hood it shows a different story. Yes, they are billing out at €500 or more per day but when they consider all costs it turns out that they aren't making a €500 profit.

We said there earlier that if you have 5 employees or less you should be aiming for €500 per day, well what if you have more than 5 employees. If that's the case you should apply the same test to your business and see if you are hitting that target. On average usually, a client who I work with can make €500 per day with himself and 3 employees.

If you have more employees you should be making more than that, but again unfortunately in my experience, most small operators are not hitting this target and if that is how you run your business, it is time to get back to basics and let's figure it all out. The goal is not to do as much work as possible. The goal should always be to make your €500 per day by doing the least amount of work.

The absolute perfect job would be if on the first working day of the year you could do 1 job that took 1 man to complete and you got 1 year's wages from that job and you knew that next year you had the same job lined up again. Of course, we are unlikely to get 1 year's wages for 1 man doing 1 day's work but if you can think in this absolute sense it would make the concept easier to understand. Whilst we are not getting this type of job, we must run our business in a manner that allows us to make an absolute clear net profit of €500 per day. This is now the purpose of your business. The type of work you do, the number of staff you hire, all of that is secondary in importance to the purpose of your business. I can make a prediction now that in the future, when you encounter some issues in your business that starts to affect your cash flow and profitability, it will all be linked back to you allowing something else to take priority over the purpose of your business.

When you start to apply these strategies to your business, at the start it can be very daunting and it can feel like a bit of a rollercoaster ride, but that's just usually because you are going about something in a completely different way than you are used to doing.

This kind of up and down is very normal for someone who has been running their business in a traditional and not very profitable way. During the learning phase, you begin to say to yourself – holy sh!t this stuff works, but you only have your past business as a reference point so for the first short while you keep reverting to this, but then after a few months, this way of operating becomes your new normal and it's not long before you want to increase your targets yet again.

To help with this I always like to get people to visualise that you are sitting at your kitchen table on Christmas day. It's an hour or so before all the family are coming over for dinner and you know one of the in-laws is going to ask you, how was the year for you. You reply it was great, but what does great mean to you. If you have not managed to knock it out of the park just yet financially, this is what I believe is a good benchmark to determine if your business has done great throughout the year or not. So, as we said you are sitting at your kitchen table, the dinner is cooking away but there is nobody in the house just yet.

On the table in front of you are two piles of papers. The first pile has maybe 20 pages in it and the second pile only has two pages in it.

The first pile is your bank statement from your current account. It has all the transactions with money going in and out of your account and the bank balance is more fluctuating as opposed to growing. However, when you look closer you can see that there is one transaction within the first couple of days every month and it is a transfer from this account to another account. It is a transfer to the company savings account.

Now we go over and look at the second, smaller stack of paper that contains only 2 pages. This account has a bank balance of €120,000 made up of 12 lodgements of €10,000 each. What we did was we took the cream off the table at the end of every month and we transferred to our savings account within the first couple of days of the month the profit from the month previous.

Depending on where you are at in your business, €120k profit per year will seem to be a lot or will seem to be not enough and this paragraph is for those who feel like €120k profit is a lot. So again, let's break it back down for you.

How €120,000 Feels To You Now:

You feel €120k profit within the year is a lot – OK,

You feel that €10k profit per month is a lot – OK,

You feel that €500 profit per day is a lot – OK

The Break Down:

To hit €10k in the month you only need to make €500 for 20 days

But you most likely work almost the full 30 days per month

You feel you can't get €500 per day but you mostly get €300ish per day.

Ok, so let's multiply €300 x 30 days, it's still bringing you close to your 10k.

If you are feeling this level of earnings is still out of your reach, I strongly believe that you are falling into the trap that most people in my area were falling into as I described in the introduction. You have not set the bar too high and now cannot reach it, you have set the bar too low and you are hitting the target.

I would strongly encourage you to raise the bar and raise your level of self-belief. The universe will give you what you want, you only need to ask for it.

From time to time there is an element of hubris with certain people during this conversation, and let's be honest we are all hard-working grafters, we are all our own boss, we are all the captains of our own ship, so when you hear someone like me advising you on how you should be running your company, sometimes it can be quite a bitter pill to swallow. And if you fall into this bracket, that's fine. I respect your opinion, but I would invite you to roll with me on this for the next while.

When you say to yourself that you are hitting your €500 per day and I then ask you if it's in the bank. You cannot say, well I bought a new van, or I upgraded my office, I invested back in the company. The €500 per day must be in the company bank account, otherwise you aren't hitting that target in my estimation. The only genuine reason you can have for not having your profits in your bank account is if you used the cash to buy an investment property.

Chapter 2

The Enquiry Book

The Enquiry Book

So once we have nailed down the purpose of our business or gotten our head around the fact that our business must have a purpose, we now need to get down to business.

As a small operator we need to understand the method that all businesses use to generate profit is either one or all of the following or even a combination of them all:

1.) They sell their own labour

2.) They sell the labour of their staff

3.) They sell the products made by their staff

4.) They sell the products they bought to sell on at a

higher profit

If you are running a micro-enterprise you need to be very aware that a good portion of the profits made by your company will come from you selling your labour or else you selling the labour of your staff of which you must spend your own personal time supervising these staff to ensure that their work is done correctly. With all of this taken into consideration, you must be very aware that one of the most important commodities you have and of which you must safeguard very tightly is your own time.

There is an attitude among the general public that they can just call up a builder or tradesman and ask him for a quote, the tradesman must then drive across the city and incur fuel costs and toll bridges, not to mention the fact that he is not doing any work in the time he has allocated to meet you. This is the normal attitude that the general public holds and it's not really up to us to change it because if we get our act together and make sure these guys are not wasting our time, you can bet your life on it that there will be a long line of tradesmen who will still allow this to happen to them.

To make sure you are not one of these kinds of guys, you must understand that there needs to be a process for every aspect of your business as without a process you will just follow whichever way the wind blows or you will end up going with the flow, and as they say the only thing that usually goes with the flow is a dead fish.

So, we are going to make sure from the absolute outset that we don't end up going with the flow and that we have a proper system in place to help us out each step of the way.

Today we are going to introduce you to the enquiry book.

The enquiry book is a simple word document that you can print off and have stapled together or bound together and you then leave this on the dashboard of your van. I have a copy of an enquiry book template available for you on my website just go to www.Joedoyle.ie/tsgfreeresources

So here is how we are going to structure all calls and enquiries for new business. Either the prospect calls you up directly or they send you on their number for you to call them back. When you get on the phone with them the first thing you say is:

"Let me just walk out to the van where it is a bit quieter and I can get my book to take some notes." This book is your enquiry book.

When you download your enquiry book you will see the questions listed in order for you to ask the client. Now here is the magical piece, there is a reason for asking each of these questions in the order they are listed. I will highlight the reason for asking each question under the actual question

1. **Date of the first call**
    (Purely for your records and file management)

2. **Can I get your name, please?**
    (Purely for your records and file management)

3. **Phone number, please**
    (Purely for your records and file management)

4. **Your email address, please**
    (Purely for your records and file management and further marketing)

5. **Postal Address**
    (Purely for your records and file management and further marketing)

6. **Can you give me a brief description of what you need to be done?**

(We ask this question to get an idea as to what they want to be done, but just as important here, we need to know where in the procurement process the client is. If they are quite vague with the details you will know that this enquiry may not be as hot as you first imagined or as hot as they are leading you to believe. This is a great question to read between the lines).

7. **Do you know when you would like to get the job done:**

(There is no point in you dropping everything and running across the city if they don't want the job done for a few months down the line).

8. **Where did you get my number from?**

(A super important question to ask in order to identify where the call originated from. If they got your number from Google, chances are the lead would not be as hot as if they said they got it from their sister for who you just finished a job for.)

9. **Can I ask how many people will be quoting for the job:**

(Just ask and generally, the clients will tell you. You have a right to know if they are looking to get 10 quotes).

10. Have you got your other quotes back in already?

(We need to know where in the procurement process the clients already are. My advice is to always be either the first quote back or the last quote. If they tell you they are still awaiting several quotes to come back to them from the other people who quoted, you need to tell them to call you back when they get their last quote back as you will be issuing them with your quote the following day as it normally takes 5 days for a quote but you are issuing quotes every day now due to you being so busy. This is going to put you in a good light as builders and tradesmen are sometimes very slow to get back with a quote and if you promise them a fast turnaround and deliver on it, they will remember it and it could improve your chances of winning the job.)

11. When I get to you on the day, I can give you a handwritten quotation while I am there, or if you prefer a printed quotation to give to a bank or credit union it will take an additional 5 days.

Remember when I said to you at the start of the chapter that we need to be able to read between the lines. If you ask this question exactly word for word, the clients will tell you either yes, they need a printed quotation in which case you know they don't have the money and are still in the process of arranging finance or, if they are not seeking finance, they will only be proud enough to tell you they don't need to be borrowing any money.

Those are the first set of questions on the enquiry book. When you download your copy, you will know that it is quite easy to follow.

The second part of the enquiry book is the follow-up page and we will get on to that now. The address to download your enquiry book template is

www.joedoyle.ie/tsgfreeresources

The Enquiry Book Part 2 – The Follow-Up:

This is a handy little tool to use to follow up with your enquiries. Again it is important to ask the questions exactly as they are worded. The worst thing you could do here is to call the clients and say hey, am I getting the job or what? If you ask that question you run the risk of them simply saying no and that's it, you are out of the running then and it could be difficult to engage in any further conversation with the client.

So, here's how the conversation should go:

Hi there, I am just following up on the quotation we issued you. Have you gotten all your quotations back?

(The reason we ask this question is to prompt a response either a negative or positive from the client about the other people quoting for the job. You can collect this data for possible use later on in the negotiations and if they told you they are pissed off about something, well you know that you better not allow yourself to make the same mistake that your competitor made.

Where did our price sit in comparison to other prices received?

(We ask this question to find out where we sit, but also to gauge the client's attitude to you (a) being the most expensive or (b) being in the middle. Never be the cheapest no matter what, if your price is the cheapest all the time you will attract a type of client who will be looking for the cheapest at all times and trust me when I tell you this, they will break your heart. If you continually get told you are the cheapest you need to increase your prices starting today).

What additional information can I get you to help you out with your decision:

(We want to appear helpful to the client at all times, notice that we did not say 'Do you need any further information to help you with your decision'? If we asked this question the client could say no, and the conversation goes cold. Simply ask what additional information I can get you to help you out. You're calling the client up, which most of your competitors have not done, and now you are asking them what you can do to help them out. This will make your company stand out and just as importantly it will make you stand out as a helpful and easy to get along with person.

Remember, in all small businesses people like dealing with people they like).

On what date do you intend to decide as to who you will be going with:

(We ask this question so that we do not need to ask them on the phone if they are going to give us the job, but asking this question generally leads the client into volunteering some information to you that they may not be willing to offer if you simply asked them 'Hey am I getting the job?'.

It's so important to understand that the reason why we are asking these questions is to (a) hopefully move them along the sales process and (b), which is probably just as important, to collect data from the engagements with the clients to allow you to improve your processes and systems so that it will drive up your success rate).

Thank you for your time. Feel free to give me a call at any time if there is anything I can help with. In the meantime, I might just send you a little video on WhatsApp to show you some other work we have done and reviews we have got from our clients.

We then sign off the conversation with this statement, in which we leave the conversation very pleasant, very helpful and also with permission to send on some further social proof to the client that they really should be going with your company. In this instance, you need to have a short video saved on your WhatsApp that will showcase some of your work but more importantly you need to showcase your reviews. So, go and screenshot your Google reviews or Facebook testimonials and include them at the end of your video. What you need to understand here is the only thing a client fears more than paying too much for a job is paying too little by going with the cheapest person and then getting a bad job done so that they need to go and redo the entire thing again. The number one thing that will put people's mind at ease is not how much you can assure them but how many other people can assure them that you are the right person for the job, so include lots of testimonials and reviews in the video you send them.

Chapter 3

Time Management

Time management

If you follow the work I do on social media you will notice that my approach is usually quite simple in that you will often shake your head and say, *'That is so simple why didn't I think of that?'*. As I write this, I did a quick Google search for 'Books on Time Management'. There are literally about a hundred of them that have popped up.

So by now, you are well clear on what the purpose of your business is, you are also clear on not having your time wasted by clients who may have had no real intention of giving you the job in the first place. The enquiry book is a mechanism to stop others from wasting your time. Now we will be discussing a mechanism to stop you from wasting your own time.

Before we dive into that we need to agree that people never really waste their own time unless of course they are lazy or distracted or suffering from a lack of focus. But hardworking motivated entrepreneurs don't waste their own time.

They do however spend their time on tasks that are not the correct use of their time. The problem with this is that the entrepreneur doesn't know this, and he is trying and trying, he's working harder and harder and doing all he can but he's simply not getting the result he wants. This chapter will be absolutely life-changing if you can manage to absorb the details in it and apply them to your business.

To access any Downloads mentioned in this book go to:
www.joedoyle.ie/tsgfreeresources

So, remember all the books on time management, I'm going to nail it for you here in one chapter.

There are a good lot of people who cannot function in the mornings until they have their coffee. I see these guys on zombie mode until they get to a garage at 9.30 or so until they get a coffee in them. Then they get their pep in their step. I'm obviously in the minority here as coffee is the world's most used stimulant and the most popular drink; personally, I don't drink it, I don't like the taste of it and I couldn't be arsed getting involved with something that I need to drink to perk me up.

My hack is a cold shower every morning. Every morning first thing I take a cold shower for 2 minutes and 06 seconds. The 6 seconds is the time it takes me to get into the shower after I have set the alarm. I would love to write an entire chapter on the benefits of a cold shower. Yes, it feels horrendous, yes I scream like a girl in the shower but by god when I get out of it, approx. 4-5 minutes after I have gotten out of bed, I am ready for the day and I am at my most alert. And I have also eaten the frog which is the title from a famous time management book that advises doing the most difficult tasks first. I think any man will agree that freezing your cobblers off for two minutes first thing every morning would class as a difficult task so that's that box checked.

Although it's not my area to tell you how to shower, I do know that it is a great productivity hack, a great health hack and it makes you feel like you have gotten a head start on the day.

I have included it here for you as an optional step to follow but the next step is compulsory and if you get this right it will transform your business.

In business, every single task can be broken down into one of three categories. They are either €10 tasks, €100 tasks or €1,000 tasks. That is tasks that you can get done for either €10 per hour, €100 per hour or €1,000 per hour. So, let's dive in a bit deeper and show you what I mean. You guys all know that I am a property investor & landlord.

I'm out doing deals and pushing to grow my business all the time. Let's role-play for a moment. Say a house has just been left empty by a tenant and a new tenant is due to move in but it needs to be cleaned before the new tenant moves in.

I have a choice to either go down and clean that house myself which I have done many times in my early years, but I don't anymore. It's not that cleaning a house is beneath me in any way shape or form. I have no issue with doing it, but I know it's a €10 task. It is a task that I can employ someone to do and they will charge me roughly €10 an hour. They might charge me €15 an hour or they may charge me €20 an hour. Either way, it is closer to a €10 task than it is to a €100 task.

In this instance, I have decided that I wouldn't clean the house and I would hire the cleaner to do the job at a rate of approximately €10 per hour. While the cleaner is there, he notices the radiator is loose from the wall and there is also a small leak coming from the bottom of it. In this instance, I have several choices. I can ask the cleaner to try and fix it for me, but he won't have the tools and chances are he has never fixed something like this before which means he will probably do more harm than good.

So rather than asking the cleaner to fix the radiator as a €10 task I can either go and fix it myself or I can hire a tradesman who will call to the property, have all the tools and get the job done in about an hour, upon which it will cost me approximately €100 per hour or thereabouts. Can I fix a leaking radiator myself? Most definitely I have done it many times in my early years but is it a worthwhile use of my time these days, maybe not?

So, on the same street where the house is and all this is going on let's say a neighbour knocked in and spoke to the cleaner and said they wanted to sell their own house and they would like to sell it to me.

In this instance, I have three choices. Either I send the cleaner down to negotiate the deal, or I send the plumber down to negotiate the deal. Chances are both of them have never done such a thing before; this is a task that has a value of more than €10 an hour, more than €100 an hour and maybe even more than €1,000 an hour. Therefore, this task qualifies as a €1,000 an hour task and as such it should be done by me personally.

You might be saying to yourself well it's different for you Joe, your company is bigger and you have the money to pay

To access any Downloads mentioned in this book go to:
www.joedoyle.ie/tsgfreeresources

others to do these tasks for you, I'm only starting off or I'm just bouncing back from a setback. To that, I have to say to you that I would not have been able to grow my business at all if I didn't adopt this approach several years ago.

When I set up my second building company, we specialised in carrying out insurance-based property repairs. I knew from day one I had to get off the tools and stay off the tools. I moved towards a supervisory role on the repairs end of things, after which I then was able to move to a position where I only needed to call to get the jobs signed off.

Eventually, I then employed staff that signed off the jobs. It was a gradual process of delegating work to allow me to focus on growing the business and it paid off. So, take on board that this transition must start for you today.

Do not clean up after your days' work and do not load the tools in or out of your van, do not go to the shop for lunch. Delegate all of these tasks to either your apprentice or your labourer; you can then go and use this time to chase up work or chase up invoices or payments. Basically, you are eliminating all €10 tasks asap.

It's a very worthwhile exercise for you to audit your day and it will show you how you are performing. Make out a spreadsheet with the time down the left-hand side in 30-minute increments and the days of the week across the top.

Now you can go and complete all of the tasks you have undertaken throughout the week. When you have the tasks completed, it is now time to categorise and colour them. All €10 tasks are to be highlighted in red, all €100 tasks are to be highlighted in amber, and all €1,000 tasks are to be highlighted in green. Stop doing the red tasks, be careful of the amber tasks and plough on with as many green tasks as possible.

€10, €100, €1,000 Task Breakdown:

A €10 task is any task that you can get done for free up to €50 per hour

A €100 task is any task that you can get done that costs you €51 up to maybe €400 per hour

A €1,000 task is any task that costs more than €400 per hour.

I enjoy the conversations I have with my clients when they realise for the first time that all the things that they have been doing in their business may not have been serving them well at all. Recently I was chatting with Vincent Hamilton of VH Plumbing & Gas from Enniskillen. Vincent and I were chatting and I asked him what he would class as one of the biggest game-changers for him since he started following my program. He said outright that it was completely down to being willing to tell people NO when they asked him to do some €10 tasks. For myself, I wasn't surprised as I have seen this many times before, but it was nice to see how such a simple shift could help this small business owner consistently hit his targets.

I find by operating on this basis it gives enough scope to understand the process and the €400 per hour rate is generally enough for a business owner to sell an hour of his time for. As your company grows, you will possibly not find it a worthwhile use of your time to sell it for €400 even though you may spend time chatting to other guys and not getting paid for it, this is usually in the hope and pursuit of additional work.

You can get a template **TIME AUDIT** spreadsheet by going to *www.joedoyle.ie/tsgfreeresources*

Many weeks before writing this book I met a builder at a house I had purchased in Ballyfermot. I had mentioned to some of my property investing mentorship clients that I was doing a visit at the house and they were more than welcome to come along for the experience if they wanted to. So, I met the builder there who was a lad called Dave and my client Max came along for the spin.

We did a walk-through on the house, agreed on the list of work and then Dave asked me to look at a few things with him as he has some questions for me. Dave is a top-class builder and he always does top class work for me, so he has my trust 100%.

On the second walk-through, Dave was asking me something when I interrupted him. I said Dave, whatever your question is my answer is YES. I trust your judgement completely so make a decision and I will back it up entirely. I walked out of the house and Max said to me – *"I see you're not doing any €10 tasks there Joe."* I replied to him *"Definitely not Max."* and we both laughed about it.

You will know that you have got the delegation aspect correct and you aren't wasting time on €10 tasks and when you find yourself looking for something to do. If you find yourself having a bit of free time to twiddle your thumbs you might think this is not right, but it is exactly what situation you should find yourself in.

As soon as we clear some space on the calendar for you, we can then add in some of the correct tasks needed to push on and grow your business. Aside from the €10, €100 & €1,000 tasks, you can split each task into *IGTs* and *non-IGTs*. These are income-generating tasks and non-income generating tasks.

You should always ask yourself when doing any task, be it a €10, €100 or €1,000 task, is this an *IGT* or non IGT? For a lot of people, they won't have a business but more of a job which they own and for that reason, it is so important that you focus all of your energy on the *IGTs* as your business develops into an actual business you can then come back and tackle the *non-IGTs* at that point. In my experience, I have found that people spend way too much time on *non-IGTs*.

To access any Downloads mentioned in this book go to:
www.joedoyle.ie/tsgfreeresources

In my eyes it's like they are painting the walls with a nice fresh coat of magnolia paint whilst the roof of the house is burning. You must be thinking at all times **SALES, SALES, SALES.**

If you do manage to delegate all of your *€10 tasks* and then you swap them for *non-IGT's* you will be swapping one devil for another and it will do you no favours. Just to be very clear, I will be listing out the difference between *IGTs a nd non-IGTs later on.*

I also forgot to mention that when you are doing your audit of *€10 tasks* and looking to delegate them, it doesn't just stretch as far as your business, you need to carry it over to your personal life as well. The more you delegate, the more free time you will have to think and plot your next move. *When CASH IS LOW, THE NON-IGTs MUST GO!*

Examples of €10 tasks

Cleaning your office

Cutting the grass

Making bank lodgements (of cheques)

Postage

Ordering stationery

Washing your car or van

Going to buy lunch

Cleaning up on site

Loading up tools

Doing your bookkeeping

Doing your own invoicing

Preparing payroll

Examples of €100 tasks
Being on the tools

Checking the bookkeeper's work

Checking over the invoices

Doing other tradesmen's work

Getting better deals on phone, internet, broadband

Building your website

Examples of €1,000 tasks
Meeting clients for jobs

Checking finished works

Meeting your accountant

Negotiating a property deal

Negotiating a lease

Buying a new van

Compiling a marketing campaign

Designing your website

Prospecting with leads for new business

Calling old clients for new business

Hiring new staff

Examples of IGTs
Being on the tools

Meeting clients for jobs

Negotiating a property deal

Negotiating a lease

Buying a new van

Compiling a marketing campaign

Designing your website

Prospecting with leads for new business

Calling old clients for new business

Examples of non-IGTs
Cleaning your office

Cutting the grass

Making bank lodgements (of cheques)

Postage

Ordering stationery

Washing your car or van

Going to buy lunch

Cleaning up on site

Loading up tools

Doing your bookkeeping

Doing your own invoicing

Preparing payroll

Checking the bookkeeper's work

Checking over the invoices

Doing work that you have already paid other tradesmen to do

Meeting your accountant

Buying a new van

Hiring new staff

As Self Employed entrepreneurs we are all guilty of holding on too tight and not just letting go so that we don't stand in our own way anymore.

When my client and buddy David O'Shaughnessy of Midwest Tiling Solutions in Co. Clare first grasped the notion of the

€10 tasks he was completely blown away. He had been running around doing absolutely everything in his business and wasn't delegating. He looked purely at the fact that why should he pay someone to do something that he can do himself.

What he wasn't looking at, at the time, was the amount of opportunity and sales he was missing by not focusing on the bigger picture. When he did get his head around this concept his business went from €200 to more than €500 a day. Here is what he had to say:

'When you can grasp the idea that your business can earn you €500 profit every day and you start to do it, you have to re-evaluate all your time.

After I began to delegate the €10 tasks, I had more time to be where I needed to be, which made the jobs run smoother. There was quicker turnaround on jobs and, in turn, the profits and business magically started to improve.' - David O'Shaughnessy.

I'm sure you will be well aware of my video called TOM THE PLUMBER. This is an animated video that tells a story of a man called TOM and how he is struggling to try to do everything in his business. Go and check it out on YouTube if you haven't seen it; I'm sure you will be able to relate to him completely. Just search for Tom the Plumber on my YouTube channel and you will see a whiteboard animation.

If you struggle to find the video, you can scan this QR code to take you to the Tom The Plumber video on my YouTube channel.

Joe Doyle Entrepreneur

Tom The Plumber Overworked and Unrewarded

Chapter 4

Issuing Invoices and
Getting Paid

Issuing Invoices and Getting Paid

The minute I start working with a client on their business, in the same way an apex predator sniffs out prey, I am all over the invoice end of things immediately. Clients have hired me to work with them on their business and then, when I start to look at their invoicing and finances, I actually can't sleep until I get a handle on it. It scares me the lack of urgency that some business owners have when it comes to their invoicing and money management.

Regardless of what you are doing in your business every hour or every day, if you aren't issuing invoices or acting in a manner to get you closer to issuing an invoice, you are in real trouble and you need to tackle this immediately. And, like the items discussed in the earlier chapters, this is not actually rocket science; it's not that difficult to do, it's just something that must be done differently from how you have done it before. So, let's dive into it and get things sorted for you.

We have the guy who issues multiple invoices per day, say a plumber doing callouts, and then we have a lad who does €50k extensions and refurbs, so there will be a difference in the process that works for them but there will be no absence of a process.

For the multiple invoices per day operator, there is only 1 way that you can correctly issue your invoices and that is by doing them at the end of every day. I know for a fact that the guy who does many callouts but does not issue his invoices at the end of every day is missing out on invoices and he is forgetting about them altogether. The reason being he is working on a volume of callouts and as such, there is no way for sure that he can guarantee that he doesn't miss out on any invoice.

This is coupled with the fact that many of these types of jobs will be labour only jobs and there will be no invoice from the suppliers to refresh your memory later on. You need to set your alarm for a certain time every day, flick through the diary and issue every invoice on that day.

How To Speed Up Your Invoicing Procedure:

I recommend you use an accounts package that has an app that you can create the invoice on your phone.

Creating the invoice is not the same as issuing the invoice to a client. So if you do a job and, for whatever reason, the job does not get finished on the day as planned, you must still create the invoice that day, but simply don't issue.

The invoice will appear on your app as not sent to your client but at least you won't forget about it. Never leave anything down to memory, always rely on the system or process you are using.

When I ask business owners what part of their business they struggle with, they usually say the admin and all that.

I then ask what area of the admin and they say the invoicing. The truth of the matter is the only reason they are struggling with the invoicing side of things is that they are simply not doing it regularly enough, even though they know it needs to be done.

If you have never issued an invoice from your phone before here's a little exercise to do. Go off and get an invoicing app downloaded to your phone and see how long it take you to create your first invoice. You can even set up a dummy client on the app just to play around with. Once you set your client up once, they are there ready to go for the next time.

If you were using this app on the regular and you had the customer already created, you would create an invoice in less than 60 seconds. So, when people get bogged down by not issuing their invoices, I genuinely feel sorry for them as it is definitely holding the business back and yet it is so simple to tackle.

If you are working on doing callouts, or if you mostly do bigger jobs but callouts as another service for different clients all the time, there is only 1 way to do your invoicing and collecting of payments.

Set up a *Stripe account* to accept payment via card, tell the client before you call out how much the charge will be, and that you need to be paid while you are there.

It's as simple as that; you don't want to be using up any unnecessary resources, chasing down money later on will take the goodness out of the job and the longer it goes on, the more likely you are not going to get paid.

I have helped countless company owners implement this system into their business; however, one company that sticks in my mind is *Kelly Refrigeration & Air Conditioning from Waterford.* When the company owner *Brendan Kelly* first joined our program, we found that he was spending so much time going back over old jobs just to check invoices and follow up payments, we knew that he wouldn't be able to move on to the next level until we sorted this out, got him set up to take credit card payments and to hold card details on file.

After a little bit of convincing from me to *Brendan* and then some convincing from *Brendan* to his clients, it soon became how the company operated and the issue of chasing money was almost eliminated from his business.

This freed up *Brendan's* time dramatically to help him drive on with the business which has definitely gone up a level or two since then, so respect to *Brendan* taking this strategy and implementing it into the business.

The reason why *Brendan's* company was fresh in my mind is at the time of writing this, he sent me a nice email to thank me for helping him with his business because when he started with me he had a 5-year time frame to buy a new house. I gave him a few gentle nudges and he managed to do it in 3 years. It's helping guys get results like this that makes the job I do so rewarding.

Invoicing For Bigger Jobs:

For companies that issue bigger invoices in the thousands and ten thousands, I always recommend that you issue your invoice on **Day 1** of the job and issue the invoice for the full contract price.

Say for example it is a €100k job. My advice would be to issue the invoice for €100k on day one and allow the clients to *pay off the invoice in instalments.*

I would also be asking them to confirm receipt of the invoice and that everything is in order with the invoice.

If you are doing what most people are doing and issuing an invoice every time you are looking to get paid, you leave yourself exposed to someone saying to you that there was an issue with the invoice and that's the reason why payment is now delayed.

Get one invoice issued at the start and let them make payments on account of that invoice. It also means that when you are going through your accounts there will be fewer sales invoices which means you will be less likely to get confused.

Getting Agreement On A Payment Schedule:

I strongly recommend that you take your profit upfront on day one with your first instalment. There is never an issue with getting paid the first instalment and the issues only ever arise later on with payments towards the end of the job. If you're doing a 60k job and you expect to make a 12k profit on the entire job. With instalments of 20k, 20k, 10k, 10k, I strongly recommend that you take 6k from both the first and second instalments and set them aside. You must take your profit first which means if there is a problem with the job (and let's face it, there is more of a risk of not getting paid in the construction game than there is anywhere else), and the clients want to hold back money, at least they will be holding back their money and not yours. Take the profit first, set it aside and once the job finishes nicely and everyone is happy, you can then spend the profit.

I have seen instances many times where there was an issue with the job and the builder goes all-in on trying to fix it, at considerable additional expense to himself as he wants to keep the client happy, only for the client to turn around and say that they want to be compensated by way of a reduction in price on account of the inconvenience.

If payments are delayed, it is usually a warning sign and I would always recommend that the minute this happens you contact the client directly and explain to them that you need to get money for the wages so if the delays aren't resolved by the end of the week that you will need to nip off and do another job and you can come back to them whenever their issues are resolved.

Be very careful not to say this in any kind of confrontational or cheeky way.

You just need to explain that you are sorry but there is nothing you can do as the money is not there to cover the staff's wages and you need to bring in some extra work to cover the cost.

Never allow yourself to get involved in a situation where you are cash-flowing other people's projects. It doesn't make a difference how long you have been working for them or how sound they are.

If you have €30k in the company account and you are owed €70k that means for you to get €90k in the bank you will need to be owed €210k based on those ratios.

The other problem with operating on this basis, where you allow yourself to be used as a bank for clients or main contractors, is that the bigger your company grows and the more profitable it becomes, the more likely it will be that all of the cash owed in will belong to the company and not be owed out. This then means that you are less likely to chase it as much as you would if you owed it out.

And the bigger you go the bigger the fall can be, so be warned. I always recommend that you operate your business based on no more than 50% of the bank balance being owed. Some business owners will think this is impossible to achieve while others will say it's no problem.

The difficulty is for the guys who believe that this is impossible to do, they do not realise that other people are already running their businesses in this fashion. I'm not saying don't issue invoices in this instance, it is the complete opposite. What I am saying is to work harder to keep some cash reserves and work even harder to get paid quicker.

Extras on works:

If you are thinking that you can't issue an invoice on day 1 of the job as this doesn't account for any extras that will be incurred, and as we know there are always extras on the jobs, and it is usually here that the issue of payment arises. Here's how I feel you can best protect yourself against this.

At the start of the job, you should get a signed agreement from the client confirming acknowledgement of the scope, price and terms and conditions. Within the terms and conditions, there should be a note to advise that it is a fixed price contract and removal of any aspect of work does not necessarily mean the price will be reduced.

It should also state that any additions to the work schedule will be done by way of a separate agreement and must be paid for in full at the time of order commencement. What this means is that the main job is the main job and there will be no variations on this, but any extra works requested will be quoted for, signed for, and paid for in full at the time of order commencement.

Let's say the job you are doing for a client is 50k and they ask you to change some lights for them at an additional cost of €2,000. The client will have no problem paying you in full for the lights at the time of order commencement if they still owe you the guts of 50k. By implementing this system there can be no confusion over costs and extras later on.

You see, when I hear people telling me about a drama on a job that resulted in them not getting paid, I view the fact that they didn't get paid not as the problem but as the symptom of something that went on earlier on in the business. Either the client was not explained to fully, or they were explained to fully, but you didn't follow it up in writing and now there is some wriggle room on the negotiation later on.

Personally, I find the most insulting thing anyone can do to a business owner is to negotiate on a job after it has been completed, and the only way a business owner can protect themselves against this is to have everything documented correctly in writing in advance of any work commencing.

A powerful line to include in any email when discussing scope or costs is – *Can you please confirm by reply that you are happy to proceed on this basis?*

If contracts and agreements are not your strongest point, I have a suite of documents called the 3 essential documents

These 3 documents are the initial site visit document, the client's work schedule document and the sign-off document.

You can access these documents by going to: www.joedoyle. ie/tsgfreeresources

We will discuss these documents in greater detail in a later chapter.

Chapter 5

Becoming A Yes Man

Becoming A YES Man

One of the biggest mistakes that I made, particularly when I began mentoring business owners, was I gave them lots of data, information and instructions and then expected them to get the same results as me.

I mean it can't be much more simple than that, can it? Here are the results that I have gotten; here's the action I took to allow me to get that result; so go and follow it and you will get the same result. Simples, or so I thought. I was completely wrong.

What I hadn't taken into consideration at any point along the way was that people are not robots, they are not logical beings who follow logical instructions. I mean we can follow logical instructions, but our primary way of operating is based on emotions and based on dealing with people that we like or have a connection with.

People like people who make them feel good about themselves, people like dealing with people with who they can have a bond or some kind of common ground with. Basically, people like dealing with sound people who they can get along with, and the easiest way to get along with someone is to be agreeable.

Be agreeable to people when they ask you to do things. If someone calls you up and asks you if you can do a job tomorrow at 9.00 am, don't tell them that you can't do the job as you have something else on. Tell them that you can do the job, the only catch is it won't be at 9.00 am and you would need to move something around for them if it is urgent or you will be able to sort it out for them at a later time.

Notice I said to him that you would need to move something around, we didn't say that you would 100% move something around for them.

Being agreeable is a great way to build rapport with someone and to let them get to like you; it's a great way to get them to choose you over someone else.

Everyone will class themselves as being busy to some degree, be they a busy professional running a business or a parent who is at home looking after kids.

In everyone's own eyes they are busy, and in everyone's own eyes they are one of the most important people in their world and they don't like being told NO.

They may be told no on the regular by different people in different situations, but they do not like being told no, and that goes for customers, suppliers, staff members, contractors. In fact, it applies to all human beings.

Think about this with me for a moment, take a random person who you interact with regularly and ask yourself what would happen if you were to call them now and ask them to do a task.

Let's say you asked them if it was possible to pick up something from a supplier on the way home from work. Their answer would start with one of the following:

1. **Outright no.**
2. **Not now, maybe later.**
3. **Not now, but later.**
4. **Yes, but not now.**
5. **Yes, no problem.**

Even if they answered with an outright No! and you then began to explain to them how important it is for you and the job at hand that they collect this product from the suppliers, chances are they would still end up doing it for you. Regardless of how they answered you, there's still a good chance that they will do this for you.

Thinking Exercise:

Now, let's say you had 2 people that you could call and ask them to do the same task and you knew that both of them would do it, but you would need to convince one of them to do it and almost beg, or insist that they do it, and the second person would answer with a Yes, no problem.

Who would you be more likely to ask first?

Chances are that you would ask the most agreeable person first.

Chances are you would find the second person more agreeable, you would find them easier to deal with, you would find them to be more of a team player and someone who you prefer to have on your team over someone who you need to negotiate with over every little thing.

We need to be very clear on something here, we are talking purely about attitude here, we are talking about the attitude you use to deal with your clients, staff, suppliers & contractors. We are most definitely not talking about you dropping everything and running every time someone springs a random task on you.

Down through the years in our building company, we had a lot of people come through the doors as staff, contractors, suppliers. In a lot of instances, we would have more than one trade with us and over time it was the guys who had the attitude of *'send me on the job, I'll squeeze it in somewhere'* that stood the test of time and were with us for a lot longer than the guys who wanted to insist on telling you how busy they were.

And when it comes to being busy, let me tell you something. It is purely a state of mind and a state of priority. We all have the same number of hours in the day and we all keep ourselves occupied every day so when someone tells you how busy they are it is not a sign of how successful they are and how profitable they are.

So bear in mind I'm coming at this from the point of view of having dealt with thousands of 'busy people' but when it comes to dealing with these types, it's usually these guys who have so much work that they don't know what to do one minute, to having no work all of a sudden.

Of course we don't want to be a busy fool, there are already enough of them out there. But we do want to be a man who in the eyes of everyone who knows him, they feel they can call him up and no matter what query they have you're going to offer them some honest, positive and valuable encouragement.

One of the greatest life lessons I have ever learned is: *'Never make someone wrong, just so you can be right'.*

If a client is calling you up and spouting off about this and that, roll with them. If they are calling you up and spouting off, most likely they just want to be heard, they don't want to be corrected. If they ask your opinion on something that you aren't fully sure of the response to give them is: *'That's something I would need to put a bit of thought into.'*

One of the most intelligent men on the planet on this subject is Jordan Peterson who is a Canadian clinical Psychologist.

He holds the view that agreeable people earn less than those who are less agreeable as they're more likely to be pushed around and overworked.

We're not going to allow ourselves to be pushed around and overworked but we are going to be agreeable.

To access any Downloads mentioned in this book go to:
www.joedoyle.ie/tsgfreeresources

Being agreeable will allow people the comfort to give you a job over someone else.

People will be happy to deal with you if they're more comfortable dealing with you than dealing with your competitor.

Remember the priority is to define the purpose of your business, after which it is down to you to.

The priority is to define the purpose of your business, after which it is then down to you to protect your time and stay away from *€10 tasks* completely and reduce as much as possible the time spent on *€100 tasks*. So, we need to keep in mind our priorities here and not allow ourselves to be distracted.

Going back to my earlier point as to why people failed to get the same level of results as I managed to achieve, it wasn't down to skillset, it was a lot down to focus and mostly down to how I dealt with people.

One of the most common things people say to me is that they admire my energy. I like to think that people follow me for my world-class business knowledge, or for the fact that I bounced back from almost complete bankruptcy to build an 8 figure property company, but no, the fuckers say they admire my energy, so was all of that in vain?

Definitely not, but people like my energy, they like my attitude and they like my relatability. Was this something I worked on?

No, it's just me and I like to make myself easy to deal with as I know it works and I would recommend you do the same.

You know the way they say never judge people; well I hate to burst your bubble, but people are judging you all the time. If you pull up to a petrol station in a Bentley well dressed, fill it up and then go into the attendant and explain to them that you have forgotten your wallet they will look at you and judge you in a completely different light than someone says the same thing but pulls up in a banger and looks as rough as a bear's arse, the attendant will have a completely different attitude about them.

The truth is that people are making micro-judgements about you all of the time. Every little interaction they have with you they are 'getting to know you better' which means they are making up their mind whether they like you or not. They are judging you, simple as that.

So, the way you can help with this situation is to help them to decide they want to deal with you by being agreeable, being a YES, I CAN man, how can I help you?

I said earlier that one of the most important life lessons I have ever learned was 'Never make someone wrong, just so you can be right'.

As I am a fairly well-known landlord in my area, people always reach out to me on social media and ask if I have any properties to rent. I don't handle this end of things in my business and I know we have a very long waiting list, so I would write back and explain that I don't have any availability, which was completely true.

However, in this instance I was making the person wrong, I was telling them no, just so I could be right. In fact, I have done nothing wrong here other than told the other person no.

So here's what we do now, rather than writing back to these people and telling them no, and sometimes the messages would go unreplied to, which again is as bad as telling people no. I set up an auto-reply with a link to a survey monkey form advising that we currently have no properties available, but if they want to complete the form we will keep their details on file.

In this instance, we were not telling the people an outright no and go away. It was more of a no, not right now but maybe in the future. Based on the volume of enquiries we get it is unlikely we can help all of these people out, but we will be in a position to help some of them out over time and hopefully, as my business grows, I will be able to help more and more.

Chapter 6

The Make Or Break Tools

The Make Or Break Board

So far, we have figured out what the purpose of our business is, we have also looked at some time management hacks with the *€10 tasks* and some time saving hacks with the enquiry book and the invoicing process. We looked a little bit at the benefits of being a YES, I CAN man.

Now we are going to look at one of the tools that is central to allowing you to increase the profits in the business and hit the target of *€500* profit per day or multiples of this.

To avoid any confusion, you must be aware that this tool is called the Make Or Break Sheet. It is a formatted Excel sheet and this is a central part of the MAKE OR BREAK OPERATING SYSTEM. We also have the Make Or Break Board. This is an actual Whiteboard that you will buy and hang on your office wall.

It is this whiteboard that must be completed every day.

For now we will look in detail at the Make Or Break sheet but later on, in the final chapter, we discuss the MAKE OR BREAK OPERATING SYSTEM.

Keep in mind there is a difference between the 2.

The MAKE OR BREAK BOARD will show you how much money you are making daily, provided you treat it no differently than brushing your teeth or taking a shower. What I mean by that is, you would not have 7 showers on a Sunday to make up for a lack of showers all week. It must be the completed every day.

Before we look at the Make Or Break sheet, we first need to look at how things are 'normally done' in a 'traditional business' and how the accountants do things and have done them for a long time.

If you are a sole trader, the law states that you do not need to file your returns and pay your taxes until **31st October** *the following year.*

The benefit of this is if you started your business on January 1st this year, you will not need to pay any taxes until the 31st of October next year. That's a full 22 months away, great for starting off and if you are worried about paying tax, but not good if you are looking to find out if you're making money or not on a daily basis.

If you are a limited company, you do not need to file your returns with revenue and CRO until 9 months after your year-end, your year-end will be 12 months after you started trading. Again, great if you are worried about paying your taxes but not great if you are trying to figure out how much money you have made in a week, month or quarter.

When we start our business it is our baby; we love, worry and care for it as if it were a child. But you wouldn't drop your child off anywhere and then not check in on them again for another 12 months.

As a business owner and entrepreneur, you need to know the score of your business every day. You need to know how much money you have in the business, how much work you have ahead of you and how much money you are making daily. If you don't, you are sailing blindly into the dark and cannot make any of the many minor regular tweaks that are needed to keep you on course.

My *MAKE OR BREAK BOARD* does away with all of that, but it is only as good as your willingness to stick to it and be warned, we are going to get a bit technical in this part. MY *MAKE OR BREAK BOARD* is a two-part tool.

The first part involves you working out your daily break-even point for the business and how much you should be charging for each of your staff daily.

The second part is a physical whiteboard that we need you to purchase and hang on the wall in your office. This board needs to be laid out in a certain way and needs to get completed daily, even if the results are zero. There are some slight variations for companies that are set up differently, but we will look at that in a minute.

When I talk to business owners about making €500 profit per day a lot of the time they think they are making that amount of money, or at least they tell me they are making that amount of money.

So, I then ask them for how long they have been making that amount of money, I then add up €500 per day by the amount of time they have told me. Based on the figures they have given me, I can then add up an approximate amount of money they should have in their account but guess what?

They rarely have in their business bank account the amount of which would equate to them earning €500 profit per day.

The problem here is leakage of some sort; they are not making the money or else they have miscalculated their overheads, or else underestimated how much downtime they have in the business.

Either way, it's not that difficult to fix but you must follow the process.

Have you ever found yourself with a few quiet days coming down the line and you farm out your staff at a rate just to cover their wages because it is better than having nothing for them to do?

On these days you are most likely losing money but just don't realise it. What you need to know is what obligations a staff member has, or should I say what obligations you have, to ensure that your staff members are hitting the correct earning capacity.

Regardless of company type, size or industry, all staff members must cover the following costs if they are to be considered as part of the team.

What Staff Need To Cover:

- Their wages including holiday pay and employer's PRSI
- Their redundancy

- Their portion of the overheads of the company

- Their portion of the desired profit of the company (which in this instance is €500 per day).

If you have 5 staff members, each of them must make you a profit of at least €100 per day after staff costs and overheads have been included.

If you have 2 staff members, the number will be €250 per day after their staff costs and overheads have been included.

I find the optimum size team is 3 staff and one working employer. I think it's worthwhile to emphasise to owners of companies who are turning over millions with razor-thin margins who must carry out a lot of work to make €100,000 profit, that 4-men crews can make €10,000 per month clear profit for the company owners.

I say this about companies turning over multiple 7 figures because, in a lot of instances, tradesmen don't realise that you can hit a profit of 10k per month. I have dozens of clients who are hitting this type of profit with 3 or 4 staff. I also want to stress this point to the small operator with 3 or 4 staff. You don't need a massive crew or a massive turnover to make 500 profit per day which is 10k profit per month based on a 20 day month.

To get your template copy of your make of break sheet go to www.joedoyle.ie/tsgfreeresources

You can compile your sheet at any time regardless of what stage your business is at.

The make or break sheet is a carefully designed formatted Excel sheet that gives clarity to the exact running costs and overheads for the running of your business without you needing to be an Excel wizard or have an accountancy background.

This Excel sheet is laid out in a certain format with space at the top to list off all your company expenses. This is then broken down into a monthly, weekly and daily figure. This is your overhead figure and it is then broken down some more, based on the number of employees that you have.

It breaks down this far so that you can determine what your hourly overhead rate per employee is by simply filling in the required info.

Make Or Break Sheet Section 2

After you have this figure, you then go and complete section 2 for each of your employees. You add in their name and their gross hourly wage. The spreadsheet then adds for employer's PRSI, holiday pay, redundancy, downtime, overheads and profit.

When you have completed section two, you then go to the top right- hand side of the spreadsheet and you will be able to see how much you should be charging out for each of your men, should you wish to make a clear profit of €500 per day.

At this point that is the MAKE OR BREAK SHEET completed. You now know what the absolute minimum amount that you must be charging out for each of your staff daily. This is your *EMPLOYEE DAILY* Break-even Point. We take this figure and we bring it over on to our MAKE OR BREAK BOARD. This is the part where people begin to veer off my instructions and they get lost and confused.

Of course, you can complete your MAKE OR BREAK BOARD on Excel or Google sheets but if you follow my instructions and get a whiteboard and hang it on the wall of your office, you will be far more likely to stick to it and you will be far more likely to get the benefits.

The Make Or Break Board:

When we get the whiteboard, we draw some lines on it with permanent markers as these lines will not need to be changed regularly. Across the top, one column out from the left, we write the days of the week. Along the left-hand side down the board, you write each of your staff members' names. At the end of each day, we write

- Total billed for the day including materials is now down how much we billed each man out for on that day. known as: **(Figure A).**

- Underneath this we write how much the materials for the day totalled up to, this is now known as **(Figure B).**

- From our MAKE OR BREAK Sheet, we write on to our board our daily break-even amount, this is now known as **(Figure C).**
- (**A**) minus (**B**) minus (**C**) will give you a figure that we call **(Figure D)**

This here is your daily profit and the goal here is that at all times you make sure that the number is always more than zero. The reason we say it is more than zero is that if you can think back you will remember that we already have €500 profit per day factored in here.

If this all sounds confusing don't worry, we have a free video tutorial in our resources for you.

The magic about this sheet is that when you make your €500 profit per day we don't show it along the bottom as €500 profit even though we know it's there. We show it as zero, and all you need to do is make sure every day that you do not have any figure less than zero.

You may not see it right now, but as soon as you get into using this daily, it will become ingrained in your brain and it will keep you awake at night if you think that you are going to end up with a minus number on the board.

I get guys sending me emails and WhatsApp messages all the time with images of their MAKE OR BREAK board and they are making more money than they ever have before, however they have a couple of minuses on the board and it's driving them nuts. If you find yourself at this stage, that means the system is working and you are doing a good job.

The other hidden secret with setting up your MAKE OR BREAK BOARD is that you can hang it up in your office where staff can see it and because it is not screaming out that you are making €500 or more every day, you won't mind your staff seeing it.

The above scenario is best suited for companies doing multiples of small jobs; if you are doing bigger jobs, only a minor tweak is needed. No matter what, you must complete column B and column C every day.

What you are missing now is the amount billed for the day including materials which will be zero if you are working with bigger jobs that take a week or a month to complete. When the job is complete you can divide the invoice amount by the number of days it took to complete the job and see what score you get from there.

This is a great test to do in order to determine if the big job is as profitable at the end as you thought it was at the start. When doing jobs that take more than one day to complete, for example, a week, a month or even six months, the most important number is not the profit on the job, but the profit per day on the job.

It is a massive awakening for many people when we work out the profit per job per day. This is also an area where you can go wrong if you are taking some advice from your accountant on what type of job to go after.

You see, the traditional method of accounting and reporting will only consider what numbers are in the accounts, but it will not give any indication on how long it took to complete a job or the hardship involved. The most important thing to be aware of is the profit per job per day. If you keep this in mind you won't go far wrong.

Throughout this book we have some resources and downloads that we want you to have for free as part of using this book, however, I cannot emphasise enough the importance of accessing and implementing the *MAKE OR BREAK SHEET* as it will give you a sense of control over the numbers and the information within your business and you will know where you stand daily.

As you start to use this sheet, I would encourage you not to get bogged down if you have not included an item on your sheet as this can always be added in later on, but we do need you to commit to being consistent and filling it in every day.

To access your template MAKE OR BREAK SHEET go to: www.joedoyle.ie/tsgfreeresources

Chapter 7

The Three
Essential Documents

Three Essential Documents

Throughout running your business, there will be so much paperwork that it will drive you nuts; some pieces of paper are more important and more valuable than others and for that reason, I want to introduce you to your Three Essential Documents.

Like the other templates referenced in this book, you can access your Three Essential Documents by going to: www.joedoyle.ie/tsgfreeresources

Before we dive into looking at these three essential documents, I want to let you inside my mind a little bit. Having been in business for so long, been sued before, people trying to get injunctions against me, trying to get money out of me and all sorts of carrying on, it makes you a little bit paranoid. Many aspiring entrepreneurs see what they believe is an opportunity and go hunting it down purely as it is a shame to let an opportunity go to waste and rightly so. However, I believe that there is opportunity everywhere and as such, I will go after each opportunity that comes my way and if I don't capture it, I know there will be another not far behind it.

However, before I get into every opportunity, I size up everything and everyone that's involved, and I look at everyone and ask myself, 'Is this guy gonna do my head in, is he gonna be a ball-breaker and cause me all sorts of hassle'. If the answer is not an absolute 100% that the guy is a good guy, well then I walk away. I think of everything in absolute extremes, I think what would I say now if I was in court and had to explain this case to the judge. You may have heard me say to people on social media and my podcasts, don't tell me anything, show me.

When it comes to business, whatever you told a client, or you claim that you told them carries absolutely no weight in comparison to what you told them in writing and what you had them sign. That's how the Three Essential Documents evolved; these documents were tweaked and tweaked over time and now they are a robust suite of documents that I recommend you implement into your business.

The Three Essential Documents work based on getting documents signed at three stages of the project. The first document gets signed at the initial site inspection; the second document gets signed before the commencement of works; this is the schedule of work which contains the list of works, the price and the terms and conditions attached. The final document is called the sign-off sheet and this gets signed at the end of the project to signal that the client was happy with the work at the end of the job. The 3 Essential Documents in their current format work perfectly for projects where it is Business To Consumer (B2C) as opposed to Business To Business (B2B), but you can review them and tweak them to your satisfaction as it will give you a good base and get you 95% of the way there.

Document 1 – Site Inspection Sheet

This is a sheet that contains all the relevant fields to complete the client's contact details and a description of their desired works.

There is a space to complete room dimensions and also a space to complete notes.

You must write clearly on the sheet and when you have taken all of the information necessary, you then hand it to the client to read over and check they were happy with it. You then ask them to initial or sign it. You advise them that this is an office procedure to avoid any staff taking short cuts and doing site meetings over Zoom and taking measurements from clients, and it proves the staff member was on site. If you are the gaffer you tell the client you implemented this system for the entire crew and as such you must follow through on the rules yourself; what's good for one is good for all in your eyes.

There is no contractual or obligatory value in the client's eyes for this document and it doesn't give you any legal standing, however in the event of some disagreement later on, it will form part of a suite of documents that were signed by the client.

Document 2 – Works Schedule

This is one of the more important documents as it contains all of the descriptions of the works as agreed with the client, it contains the price and most importantly it contains the terms and conditions to which the client is agreeing to. I won't get into it here what each of the terms and conditions are, but it contains 10 years of revisions to make things tighter and tighter in your favour and to remove any scope for confusion or ambiguity later on. Never start a job or agree to a price with a client verbally until a work schedule is signed. If you are dealing with a client over email as discussed in an earlier chapter be sure to send the email to the client with the work schedule pasted into the email and not attached. Specifically, state within the email the following words:

Can you please confirm by reply that you are happy to proceed on this basis?

This allows the client to write back a one-word answer being a 'YES' and there can be no confusion later on. If you send the works schedule as an attachment and you do find yourself standing in the literal or proverbial witness box later on, it is more difficult to explain what the attached contains (trust me I have been there before), whereas if you can just show a full string of emails it reads much better and it is easier to get your point across. This works particularly well in situations where you have to take a client to court for non-payment.

Document 3 - Sign Off Docket

This is a very simple docket type document that you get the client to sign at the end of the job. It states on it specifically in capital letters right next to where the client is asked to sign:

DO NOT SIGN THIS DOCUMENT UNLESS ALL WORKS ARE COMPLETED TO YOUR SATISFACTION

This brings closure to the job and a client will not sign it unless they are happy with the job. This doesn't guarantee you will get paid and doesn't protect you against the client complaining later on, but it does show that on that date the client was happy with the job. This is a very useful document when a client is trying to avoid paying you and claiming that it is a result of faulty or incomplete works. It shows at that date the client was happy to class the job as signed off.

For smaller jobs, if you are working on that basis of collecting payment via credit card and they have already paid you via Stripe which means your system already holds their credit card details, it can include a line of text that confirms upon signing that the client gives permission for you to charge the card held on file. Having a signature on file for a client who is paying you via card is a very powerful piece of evidence in the event of the client doing a chargeback with their card company.

The other item to take into consideration here is that you are probably the only company that has requested that the client sign several documents, and one document at every stage. This will set you apart from the competition and will result in less drama and less potential issues arising from the works. If there is any grey area in the paperwork and a client is looking for a reason to complain, they will complain; by having the paperwork very tight it improves matters overall for both parties and gives messers less wriggle room and, to be honest, I have found that messers simply go somewhere else when they realise they are dealing with someone who is running a slick operation.

You can access your three essential documents by going to: www.joedoyle.ie/tsgfreeresources

Chapter 8

Delivering
A Quote To Your Client

Delivering A Quote To Your Client

The first call-out & delivering the quotation.

At all times throughout the running of our business, we must be operating on the basis that everything we do gives us the best possible opportunity of securing profitable work. I have said already that the clients are judging you at every interaction. The clients are concerned if they make the wrong choice. They are concerned if they pay too much for the job and feel like they got ripped off and they are even more concerned about not paying enough and getting a bad job done.

With all of this in mind, we must do as much as possible to put their mind at ease. When you get to the point in the conversation that a call-out is required to survey the job for the first time, this is the process you must follow.

You call to the property at the mutually agreed time. You arrive on time in your branded vehicle. You wear Snickers type work trousers and boots with a polo shirt with your company logo on the left-hand side and your name printed on the right-hand side.

If you are purely in a sales role, you may not wear Snickers trousers, you might wear jeans. At all times arrive in your van, do not arrive in the 'wife's car' because you don't feel like driving the van. If you have a car that you drive for work, make sure it looks like the type of car the company would own.

There is no harm in driving an old or slightly battered van, just make sure that it is clean and make sure there are no piles of paper and rubbish scattered across the dashboard. Go and check for just a moment and see what the dashboard of your van looks like when viewed from the front. It drives me mad when I see a van with a cluttered dashboard as it is one of the first impressions a client gets when you pull up to their house.

When you do get to the door, you will be holding a small presentation folder with your company branding on the inside and out. Inside this presentation, in the folder should be your site inspection docket as mentioned in the Three Essential Documents. There should be a couple of pages of a leaflet with information about your company, your business card and also, if you can include some type of promotional keepsake item like an air freshener or pen or something along those lines. We used to leave a 30 cm school ruler with our logo printed on it.

You carry out your survey and leave the pack with the client taking back with you only your completed site survey sheet which they have now signed or initialled. The reason we say initial is if we ask them to sign it they may get funny, so the initial is purely the acknowledgement that you were there.

Depending on the job you either give them the quotation whilst you are there or else you agree on a date which you will have the quotation back to them.

Depending on the size of the job will depend on how the client reacts from here on in. If you have met one family member and the job is €5,000 or less, the other family member who was not there who is usually the man in my experience, may have the lady of the house do the research and get a couple of quotes.

When the man of the house arrives home he will ask his wife how she got on, she may say some of the other guys didn't turn up or maybe they did, either way, there is a good chance that they will not have left a nice little presentation and information pack with the client. The wife will pass comment on the other tradesmen who called to the property and then she will show your pack to the husband.

The husband only has the verbal information on the other two (let's say that she was getting 3 quotes) but he has verbal information on your company including the presentation pack. Assuming you held yourself well in the meeting and came across as a YES, I CAN man, chances are that you have dramatically improved your likelihood of winning the job.

You now need to head off and prepare a detailed quote if they have opted for a printed quote. Or, if they have opted for a handwritten quote, I would strongly suggest that you follow up with a printed quote either way. Just remember the only reason why we asked them if they wanted handwritten or printed was to see if they had the finances available.

If you give them a handwritten quote but follow up with a printed quote, this would work well for your company image.

This next part is absolutely crucial, and you need to realise that there are so many hard-working tradesmen losing out on jobs purely by how they deliver the quote to the client. You will remember from earlier-on when we discussed the enquiry book, now we are going to look directly at the process of giving the quote to the client.

When you have your quote done, call the client and ask them when it is suitable to call out and go through some details on the quotation. Be sure to make an appointment for a time when both of the homeowners are present. You may need to do this at an unsocial hour but do it nonetheless.

I find if we are talking to the husband we can jokingly say that the boss should be there also (meaning the wife), but if you are talking to the wife and you say you want to meet when the boss is home, there is a good chance you're not getting that job.

Either way, meet with the clients, bring 3 copies of the quotation and offer to walk around the house one room at a time and address each line of the quotation while standing in the room. Of course, if you are building a new house or extension there will be no rooms available so you will need to refer to the architect's drawings. During the meeting, be sure to ask the questions as listed in section 2 of the enquiry book.

Enquiry Book Template Questions:

1.) Have you gotten all your quotations back?

YES   NO   Other? _____

2.) Where did our price sit in comparison to other prices received?

_____

_____

3.) What additional information can I get you to help you out with your decision?

_____

_____

4.) On what date do you intend to make a decision as to who you will be going with?

_____

_____

If for whatever reason the clients don't want to meet up with you as they are simply not around, arrange a time so that you can call them up to discuss the quote.

1. *Ask them when they will be sitting in front of their laptop.*

2. *Tell them you will call them at their agreed time.*

The client will assume you are going to email them the quote ahead of the call, but under no circumstances should you email them a quote until you are chatting to them on the phone or even on Zoom. When you get on the phone or Zoom, ask them outright question No.1 above. When they have answered the question send the email to them while you are on the phone and tell them to open it up.

When they open it up, go straight to the price with them and ask them question No.2 above. Gauge their reaction and only then should you start to discuss the details of the quotation.

The real trick here is to make sure that by showing your attention to detail at every stage of contact with the client, you want to take them away from being hypersensitive to the price and you want them to warm to you and your approach to business.

When you go into this meeting with the client, either in person or over the phone, be sure to know what your minimum desired outcome is. I would recommend that the minimum you expect is to find out:

1. **Where your quote sits in relation to other quotes**

2. **What date they expect to decide on who they will be awarding the job to**

Obviously, the best possible outcome for yourself would be that they agree to give you the job. Business owners are usually well aware of what the ideal outcome is for themselves but very often they don't know what the minimum acceptable outcome is. It would be no harm to have this written somewhere so you can review it.

If you missed the earlier download of the enquiry book you can access this by going to www.joedoyle.ie/tsgfreeresources

Chapter
9

The Company Bank Accounts

The Company Bank Accounts

You will hear many people discuss different systems and hacks to help you manage your bank accounts. The reason I tell people to set up their accounts in the way we will discuss shortly is that I see tradesmen all the time getting into trouble and falling behind with their taxes. They look into their bank account see a lump of money and they think all is fine, but in a lot of instances, the money in the account is not theirs, it belongs to Revenue.

Or they look into their bank account, see a lump sum of money, say 50k and it is theirs and they think all is fine. However, when we take into account the time it took for them to save up this 50k, which may have been 10 years, we can now see that they are only increasing their company bank balance by 5k per year which is quite poor. This is usually caused by lads getting comfortable with seeing the lump sum and they then start taking their foot off the pedal. This is why we reduce our trading account back down to our 'ZERO' (not an actual zero as you will see in the next paragraph) every month or on every milestone date, which is usually every 7 weeks, we will look at this in detail in the chapter on the Make Or Break Operating System.

Setting Your ZERO:

People have so many varied spending habits; some people stop spending money when their bank account gets to zero, some people stop spending when they hit their credit card limit, some people don't want their bank account to drop below a certain amount, be it 5k, 10k or 100k. Either way whatever the number is that these people stop spending at is what we call their ZERO.

We need you to determine what the ZERO of your business is. I usually suggest somewhere between 2 & 3 months reserves depending on the business. The ZERO should be set at such an amount that if it dips below, you get uncomfortable, and not so high that when you look at your account you feel relaxed. We don't want you to be in the survival zone all the time but we equally don't want you in the comfort zone at the same time.

For this reason we must regularly bring our bank account back down to our ZERO. The easiest way is to do it monthly, however with my own business mentorship clients we have found that setting aside on our milestone dates which is 7 times per year is the most effective.

It's important to understand that having you set up your accounts in this way is purely applicable to small businesses operating in the construction space.

If you are a sole trader you must have *4 bank accounts* and *3 bank accounts* if you are a **limited company**. If you are a limited company you will already have a *separate personal account into which you pay your wages.* So, effectively, it is 4 bank accounts needed regardless of business set up. If you're a Limited Company

- Use accounts 1- 3. If you are a sole trader - *Use Accounts 1- 4*

Your 4 Bank Accounts:

Bank Account No. 1: Trading Account

The first bank account is your normal trading account. This is where all the money gets lodged and where all the bills get paid from.

Bank Account No. 2: Tax Account

The second account is your tax account. Every time you make a lodgement to your trading account you must immediately transfer to your tax account the VAT amount charged on the lodgement you just made. You will also be making a transfer to this account every week for any tax deducted from employee's salaries and any withholding tax deducted from contractors.

How it works is, if your employee's weekly gross is €1,000 per week and he walks away with €700 net, every week when you do your payroll run you should pay the €300 over to your tax account. You pay your taxes to your tax account as you incur them as opposed to when they fall due.

The biggest threat to your business not succeeding, regardless of what anybody is going to tell you, is that you do not make enough sales, or you do not make enough sales with enough profit on it to make sure that your business can last and can survive.

After that, the next biggest reason your business is likely to get into trouble is that you don't pay your taxes. And people get into trouble with their taxes by not doing this exercise and by not being disciplined. If you stick to this practice, you will never get in trouble with your taxes.

A new company owner will take this message on board and he will just roll with it because he knows no different, whereas someone who has been around the block a long time is more likely to offer some resistance to this way of operating. The experienced business owner might say, well that's all well and good but what happens if the cash is not there. Ok, so let's look at that. Say a contractor does a job for you for €1,000 and he is on a zero % deduction rate. When he calls to your office to get paid, you will pay him the €1,000 with no questions asked, but what happens if he is on 20% deduction.

What happens to that extra 20% that you never paid him. The truth is it gets absorbed by the trading account and gets spent elsewhere because it hasn't been managed properly.

Take for example an employee who is a single guy on a €1,000 gross per week and when you pay him he nets €700 per week. If we contrast him against another fellow employee who is also on €1,000 gross per week but because he's married and has a gang of children, his tax credits are higher, so he takes home €850 per week. In all the above scenarios you never have the opportunity to leave the employee or the contractor short without it causing a lot of hassle, so you simply don't do it.

But because you don't have to pay the Revenue on the same day, you are then not managing this piece of the money correctly.

In the above example we have tackled PAYE and contractor withholding tax, so what about VAT? It's the exact same: when you were pricing the job you priced it for what you needed to charge and then the VAT got added on top. Therefore, you didn't need it at the time and there is no reason why you should need it now. Or let's take the guy who is just starting off in his business. He doesn't charge VAT and therefore he never collects it because he is below the threshold, so when he does start to collect it, he should have no issue setting it aside just like when he never had to deal with it.

What you need to take on board here is that your current financial position is purely down to habits, of which up to now, are possibly what I would class as 'not in line with wealth creation and good business practices'. Habits can only be changed by discipline and nobody can discipline you.

So when cashflow is tight it is tight because your cash collection systems are not up to scratch. It is not that people are slow at paying it is purely that you have allowed a situation to arise where they could become slow at paying.

The magical thing about operating on this basis is that paying your PAYE and contractors withholding tax will just happen by direct debit from your tax account. But when you are paying your VAT you are going to be in a position where you have overpaid on VAT because of the VAT paid on the materials you purchased. This will mean you will be due a refund from your tax account every time you do a VAT return. You simply transfer from the tax account back to the trading account the amount which you will have paid on materials throughout that period.

Bank Account No. 3: Savings Account

The third account is your company savings account. We are going to be making a lodgement to this account every month or on every milestone date of which there are 7 in the year.

We will look at the milestone dates in more detail when discussing the *Make or Break Operating System.*

Bank Account No. 4: Wages Account

The fourth and final account is your wages account. If you are a limited company you will already have this one set up, but if you are a sole trader you may not have it set up so you must do it right away. It is not law for you to do it, but it is good practice as you will see later on.

Why Use Your Bank Accounts Like This?

If you're a sole trader, because the law will allow you to put all the money into your personal bank account, you need to be even more careful. Open up the first bank account, which is the trading account, where all the money gets lodged to. Open up the second bank account for all the taxes. Open up your third account, which is your savings account. You must take a wage from the main trading account by transferring it into your wages account. The wages account is the fourth account here. Never, ever, ever spend money directly from your trading account. The number of sole traders that do this and causes them hassle later on is huge. The reason why it causes hassle is when you go to your accountant and you're missing some invoices, he just puts them down as they were earnings for you. That's what he's supposed to do.

As a sole trader, if there is an expense out of one of your accounts and there is no invoice to match it, the accountant will allocate it as wages that you took from the business and this is not a situation you want to find yourself in.

If you implement this system you can check back at any time to see exactly how much salary you have taken. If you know that you've taken €500 every single week, and you've taken that from your trading account into your wages account, and you've spent your wages from there, you will know you've done €500 a week by 52 weeks, that's 26 thousand net.

If your accountant informs you that you've made 50 grand, you're going to ask him where the balance is and he can go back and check. It's a way for you to keep a good tight check on where you're spending your wages. If you do it this way, you will have complete transparency at all times, and you're never likely to get caught off guard.

I ask lads all the time, how much of a wage do you take, and they say I don't really take a wage. The truth of this matter is they are definitely taking something and most likely they are taking far more than they realise.

You need a correct paper trail for all the money that you spend as a sole trader to make sure it never gets allocated as earnings. I cannot stress that enough. You will make your money on doing the work, you will lose the money on not having the correct paper trail.

The one big exception to the above system is if you are a small plumbing contractor and supplying materials yourself because the materials are such an expensive part of the invoice, you will find yourself having paid a lot of VAT on these materials and, without even setting aside the VAT element of your lodgements, you could still find yourself in a situation where you are due a VAT refund from Revenue.

I have broken each part of these bank accounts down for you on a step by step basis and I know for sure that you are most likely in agreement that each step can be done. However, when it comes to implementing the entire system, you are nodding your head and saying to yourself – that's easier said than done. And you know what, you are dead right. Of course it's easier said than done but that's what it's all about. It's about putting the time, energy and discipline into making it happen and turning your business into a well disciplined, well-oiled cash producing machine.

Chapter
10

Taking A Wage
As A Business Owner

Taking A Wage

It always shocks and disappoints me when I hear of the number of business owners and self-employed people who don't take a wage from their business. No matter what stage your business is at you must take a wage, it can always afford to pay you a wage. It may not be able to afford to pay you a big wage, but it can afford to pay you something, even €100 a week, even €50 a week. Too many people make the mistake of not taking a wage at all, and we don't want to fall into that trap. You must start as you mean to go on.

Take a wage from day one. Never make the mistake of thinking, *"When I get to this point, I'll be able to take this action, and when I get to that point, I'll be able to take that action."*

Whatever you believe you want to do, or you can do in the future, you can do it today but on a smaller scale. If you want to have a wage of five grand a week, that's great, let's work towards that, but don't take zero between today and the day you get to five grand a week.

Take a weekly wage of €100 or a wage of €50. Start as you mean to go on and take that wage from day one. You should be set up on the payroll to take a payment from your business account into your personal account on the regular, like any other staff member. After that, then it's just a case of increasing it as time goes on.

As I said, the wage can increase over time, but you must take the wage, starting from today.

If you are a sole trader, never take the wage from your trading account. The law will allow you to take your wage from the trading account if you're a sole trader, but I never want you to do that. If you are a limited company, you take the wages from your limited company into your personal account, but you must never take a wage from your trading account if you are a sole trader. Pay the wage from your trading account into your dedicated personal wages account, as discussed in The Company Bank Accounts chapter.

You must take the wage, even if you don't need it, even if you are asking yourself the question, "What am I going to spend it on?" Take the wage, no matter what, I cannot emphasize this enough. And don't bring into play, "Well, sure, there's no point in paying the tax on it." Trust me, get your head around this sooner rather than later. Take the wage from the start and pay the tax on it.

I find all too often when I am chatting with new clients, up until then they have been keeping their wage below the higher rate of tax, which is currently €35,300 for single people with no children, if you have a child it's €39,300. Nobody ever got rich by avoiding paying the higher rate of tax. It's an absolute fact of the matter. Nobody got rich by avoiding paying the higher rate of tax, so do not allow entering into the higher tax bracket be the obstacle to taking a wage. You just have to pay the tax. The sooner the better, you get used to it.

The wages have to go from the trading account via an electronic transfer to your wage account. At this point, you will have your wage account set up. I can't emphasize enough, do not take it from your trading account in any way, shape, or form. Transfer it to your wage account. The only income that you should have in your wage account is the income from your business, this way it will be very easy for you to go back and check at the end of the year how much money you took.

Too many people never take a wage and find it hard to get out of that habit. They find that they start having difficulty getting their head around paying the tax. They think it's better to leave the money in the company at the higher rate rather than taking it out. Take the wage from day one. Always remember, you are your most valuable employee and you should be rewarded accordingly.

You will need to hire somebody to process your regular payroll. The way the payrolls are working nowadays, you have to report them to the Revenue in real-time which is another cost that we just need to get on with. Get it done, sooner rather than later.

If you are fortunate enough to find yourself in a position where you genuinely do not need the wage, but the company is low on cash, what you must do is still take the wage as normal and then you can lend it back to the company as a director's loan. As you transfer the money back into your company, it will then be recorded as a director's loan and you can take this money at any point in time, tax-free. Of course, the main condition being the money must be there.

It's not great practice in my opinion to leave lots of money sitting in the company account if it is owed to you as a director's loan.

Remember, the purpose of the business is to make you a profit of €500 per day or multiples of €500 per day. Over time, as the business grows, you can then use the business as a vehicle for wealth creation.

Chapter
11

**Using Your Business As A
Vehicle For Wealth Creation**

Using your business as a vehicle for wealth creation

You may have heard me say before that you must use your business as a vehicle for wealth creation, so let me share some insights with you on that. I hold a firm belief that the first step towards creating wealth comes in the form of making your business perform at a level where it will generate a clear and absolute profit of €500 per day.

The reason why we settle on this amount is that €500 profit in a single day is very achievable for guys who are either supplying labour and materials or are selling their labour plus the labour of their staff.

To make €500 in a single day is not that much of a difficult task for any tradesman even if he thinks like a tradesman and not a business owner.

The difficulty is when you try to consistently make €500 per day every single day. To do this, you need to shed your old way of thinking and you now must start to think like a business owner. You must start to think and operate like a true entrepreneur and not just a tradesman who now has a couple of lads working for him.

The unfortunate thing is that most tradesmen go through their entire working career without even realising that it is possible. If you make this transition from tradesman to business owner, chances are before long you should be able to start making a clear profit of €10,000 per month.

To access any Downloads mentioned in this book go to:
www.joedoyle.ie/tsgfreeresources

If you get to this point and you can do it for 90 days consecutively you need to pat yourself on the back because you are now well on the way to being a business owner and not just a tradesman.

The reason why we say do it for 90 days (3 months) is that by following the strategies in this book anyone can do it once, and maybe the second was a fluke but if you do it 3 times, it's now official that you know how to do it.

The crazy thing is that when you have done this for 90 days you are most likely not going to pat yourself on the back. You will be frustrated because you know you can do even more.

At this point in time, my job is to get you to cool the jets and stack 10k per month into the bank account for 12 months. When you have a full 120k set aside only then should you start to push for even more growth, the reason we work on this basis is that I believe you should be adequately rewarded by your business at each level.

You should have adequate cash reserves to cover you in the event of things not working out the first time around when we push to go on to the next level.

What is the next level I hear you ask?

Once a tradesman has now progressed along these lines and has managed to stack 120k of reserves in the savings account, I will always encourage him to do it again one more time. Having 240k in the bank is more money than most self-employed people will ever see in their life, so we get it to that point after which then there are 2 options, either clear your family home mortgage or buy a rental property.

When you do the sums on it, it usually works out that it is better to buy the rental property via a company structure and use the profit from the rental property to pay the monthly mortgage repayments on your own family home.

We won't go into company structures here in this book, but I'm happy to offer some guidance if anyone needs some help. Just drop me a mail to jd@joedoyle.ie and I will be happy to point you in the right direction.

After we get the business on point we then use the business as the vehicle to generate some cash so that we can buy more properties that eventually replace the income from the business.

How I do it:

I'm of the firm belief that businesses are usually temporary, they don't last forever and in most cases, the business is the man behind the business so as soon as he loses interest the business will decline.

Long term buy and hold property, on the other hand, that's going to be around for a long time, so my advice is to grab hold of as much of that as you can. What I am about to say might come across as 'well that's easy for someone in your position Joe'.

At the time of writing, it's been 18 years since I bought my first property and it took a long time for me to get to where I am today but looking back it shouldn't have taken so long. The way we run things is any income generated from my business never gets spent on anything other than running costs & property purchases.

Running costs are kept quite low. I take a token salary from the business but we are using this business to stockpile cash to make property purchases. For example, the sales proceeds from this book, my business mentorship program, my property mentorship program, private one to one consultancy it all gets stockpiled and we pay our base running costs from these fee's but after that, it gets used purely to purchase a property.

We then take the cash from the rent and we use this to fund my lifestyle and the running costs of the office and anything that may be due. Some people may disagree with this structure, but I like it because once I buy a property once, I own it forever and I can rent it forever. If sales drop on the business side of things, I can live with that and it doesn't affect my quality of life.

I have had people challenge me before to say that it could be seen as a lazy way of operating a business because all other business owners don't have this luxury, they need to make their business perform so they can eat. Whereas I like the fact that my income comes from my investments as it allows me to treat everything else like a game. Writing this book is a game in my eyes. Running a marketing campaign to get sales for my mentorship program is a game. Helping people turn their business around and helping them make more money it's all a game to me and if I am honest it's great craic.

I have been threatening to write this book for so long and I kept getting distracted from my 'game of writing a book'. So, I decided to rent a big villa in Spain and eliminate all distractions. I got out of bed this morning and wrote a chapter, waited for the hottest part of the day to up my fitness 'game' and went out for an 80-minute run in the heat, came back and cooled off in the pool.

Then I jumped back on here to tackle this chapter. It's 5 pm in the day and I haven't eaten yet because I have been so immersed with my work so now I have two options either eat some food or push on not eating food and complete a 36 hour fast which is also part of my health and fitness 'game'.

Now I'm a bit closer to having the book complete, to me I believe life is a game, but not a game for joking around, but a serious high- level game with great prizes and rewards. I tell people I class myself as an athlete in the sport of wealth creation.

This is a game I love so when someone is trying to compete with me as part of their job and I'm competing as part of a game. There is no way they can beat me.

I believe this ability to view your businesses and your wealth creation activities as a game only arises when you make such progress to the point that you get away from survival mode, you get away from worrying about having money to pay the wages at the weekend.

I have been in survival mode many times before and I work just as hard in game mode as I do in survival mode, but I just don't like that feeling so I do all I can to make sure I stay away from there.

How I do that is by living within my means and keeping on top of things, I don't take any unnecessary risks in business or with my investments. I run as tight a ship as possible and always stay on the side of getting rich for sure, over get rich quick, but at times I do get frustrated as I feel I am capable of a lot more.

Chapter 12

Sole Trader
Vs. Limited Company

Sole Trader Versus Limited Company

The million-dollar question that goes around in so many people's heads particularly when they are starting out is what route should I go down: Sole trader or limited company.

Sole Trader:

A sole trader is you personally. This means that when you do any work, it's you personally doing that work and carrying it out in your personal capacity. You personally assume responsibility and liability for everything. So, if something goes wrong it's down to you as the person to rectify the matter or you could be held personally liable.

Limited Company:

A limited company is a separate legal entity it is not you, it is an entity owned by you. Think of it this way, if your company owns a property you cannot live there rent-free because you don't own the property your company owns the property so you must pay rent to your company, and revenue looks at all these types of transactions very carefully.

The limited company at the end means limited liability in that the liability cannot stretch beyond the lifespan of the entity, there are a few exceptions notably if you act dishonestly or fraudulently you could be held personally liable, but they are extreme cases. So, for example, if something went horribly wrong and there was a bill of €100,000 imposed upon a limited company, but yet it didn't have it, well, then the company can't afford it.

Whereas, if it was you personally, they can just keep coming after you, because eventually, you would get the money one day.

Whereas, with a company, if it can't afford it, the company itself can be liquidated. That means it's done away with, it's gone.

There's no more that can be done in terms of chasing that company for the money.

The limited company is owned by its shareholders, which is you. You are not the limited company. You just happen to own the shares in the company. Never sign a personal guarantee for anything in the company, it defeats the purpose of it.

Sometimes you hear of people signing personal guarantees to open accounts with suppliers or banks. This just completely defeats the purpose of having the limited company. So never sign these guarantees, never sign a personal guarantee for anything in a limited company.

If you're starting off today, go limited today from the very start.

Start as you mean to go on.

Chapter
13

Let's Talk About Tax

Let's talk about tax

First off I am not a tax expert, I am purely a man who has been paying a lot of tax for a long time so you will need to check with your accountant anything that we cover here, also tax rules and regulations change all the time so what's relevant now, may not be relevant in the future.

We could spend forever and ever and ever talking about tax but now we're going to cover it in a few pages. Most people feel the biggest threat to their business is not paying tax and the tax man coming after them, but the biggest threat to your business is not generating enough sales that contain enough profit to allow your business to survive.

After sales the next biggest threat to your business is non-payment of tax. We all have accountants that are specialists in taxation and they should keep us on the straight and narrow but we just need to know a little bit about it ourselves.

Tradesmen regularly say to me – *'I'm just not that clued into the office side of things'.*

I dig a bit deeper and ask what exactly they mean, when they say the office side of things.

Usually they say the paperwork end of things.

So I dig a bit deeper when they say the paperwork end of things.

Really what they are concerned about is invoicing and keeping up to date with their taxes. We covered the invoice end of things earlier on so now we will look at the taxes.

The Different Types Of Tax:

There are many different types of taxes. We have an income tax, which is PAYE, PRSI, and then a few years ago they dreamt up a new tax they forced us to pay called USC or universal social charge. These are taxes that need to be paid by individuals, not businesses or companies. They are however deducted from the income due to the individuals by the company which is the law.

Income tax comprises PAYE, PRSI, and USC. It's typically 50% when you add them all together.

At the time of writing this, it's 40% for PAYE. Then you got 4 % on PRSI and USC varies from .5% up to 8%. To keep things simple call it half. That's all you need to worry about right now. It's half.

You do get a tax credit, in which case a certain amount of your income is taxed at 20%. And that's up to the first €35,300. But to be honest, just allow income tax as half and try to get your head around it as soon as possible.

Income Tax:

As a sole trader, your *income tax* for one year needs to be paid by October 31st of the next year. Let me say that to you again. Your income tax needs to be paid on the *31st of October* for all of the money earned in the previous year. So, it's not that year, it's the previous year.

So that means you get to earn for a whole year, and then you've got a full 10 months before you get your act together and pay your tax. For sole traders, that's a big deal because they can earn the whole year and then you've got 10 months the next year to sort it out. If sole traders could understand that this would probably make them relax about tax a little bit more.

Tax is deducted from the salary of all staff on a weekly or monthly basis, whatever way you pay your staff. If you've got staff, you should be deducting that from their salary on a weekly or monthly basis. And then we want you to send this payment over to your tax account and you can pay it to the revenue from there.

As we explained earlier on, at the time of paying our staff we immediately set aside this tax payment. We put it into our tax account and we then pay it to the revenue from there when it's due. This tax is called a P30 return and is usually paid every two months.

VAT:

The next bit of tax that we'll be all familiar with is VAT. Value-added tax, which is typically 13.5% for supply of services or 23% for supply of materials in Ireland. There are other VAT rates but we won't go in to that now. VAT is pretty much a neutral tax. You take the money in and you pay it back out. It shouldn't cost the company any money at all whatsoever. Any VAT you're paying you have already collected from the clients, so it's not your money in the first instance. VAT is a tax added to goods and services. You charge it to your client, and you pay it on the materials which you buy.

The materials you buy will be less in terms of costs than what you would charge to your client. You charge your client typically at 13.5%, but you pay it on materials at 23%. When it comes to doing your VAT return you deduct what you have paid on the materials from what you've collected from the client and you pay the balance to the revenue.

If you charged €2,000 in VAT and you've paid €800 VAT in materials, you deduct the €800 from the €2,000 and then you pay the balance of the €1,200 over to the revenue.

Once you get your head around it, VAT is quite simple at this level. It can get complex later on, but that's pretty much all that we need to know about the VAT. You take it in, you pay it back out. The law states that you must register for VAT after you've hit the threshold, which is €37,500 if you supply labour only. If you supply materials, the VAT registration threshold is €75,000.

My suggestion is to register for VAT today and start as you mean to go on. If you're ready to grow the business and drive it forward and you're going to be doing more than 75 grands worth of work a year, you may as well just get registered today and crack on as you are today. The whole notion of when I get to here, I'm going to do this, or when I get to this point, I'm going to do that, that holds you back. Start today as you mean to go on is my advice at all times. It's quite simple to register for VAT. You can do it yourself, or you can get your accountant to do it for you.

If you have been in business for any length of time you should definitely have an accountant. Instruct him to register for VAT right away if you are not already registered. If he tells you not to register for VAT, it's just because he doesn't believe that you're going to get to that level.

As we discussed earlier, every time you make a lodgement to your business account, you must then transfer the VAT amount of that lodgement into your Tax bank account. This is not the law and it is not the rules. It's how I recommend you conduct your business to avoid getting into difficulty later on.

RCT Tax:

The next type of tax that we're likely to be dealing with is RCT or Relevant Contractor's Tax. This can be applicable at 0%, 20%, or 35%. This is a withholding tax that you, as the main contractor, must withhold from any payments that you are due to make to any subcontractors who work for you.

Revenue has things pretty much tied up as much as possible now; you are not allowed to make payment to any contractor until you tell revenue. No payment can ever be made to a contractor until you put the details of the payment to be made into the revenue system, which is called ROS.

The ROS system will then tell you how much to deduct from their payment. They may tell you to deduct 0%, but you still need to process the payment through ROS. They may tell you to deduct 20%, or they may tell you to deduct 35%. The amount that they tell you to deduct has nothing got to do with you and it's entirely got to do with the contractor himself and is based on how on top of his affairs he is with revenue. It's not up to you. It's the law.

The issue with RCT is that it's a manual exercise that must be done by you or by someone in your office, on a computer every time you want to make a payment to a contractor. If you make a payment today and then you want to make another payment tomorrow, you must go and do the same thing again tomorrow because the deduction amounts can change.

If you pay a contractor the wrong amount of money, revenue will still want the tax from you. If for example, you pay a contractor 80% because you believe that you should have deducted 20%, and then revenue says you should have deducted 35%, revenue will want 35%.

There's no getting out of this. You need to be very, very careful with that. Never believe a contractor if he tells you he's on 0% or 20% you must check every single time.

Every time that you make a deduction of RCT from the payment due, you must transfer the deducted amount over to your tax bank account to pay the revenue from there like what we discussed with the other taxes.

If we just flick back here to what we discussed in the chapter on setting up your bank accounts. We may get some people reading this and they might say, "Oh, well, what if you can't afford it?"

If you were paying one of your key employees €1,000 a week, and that's gross and he's getting €700 net, and you're saying you don't have the extra €300 to set aside each week: what would happen if he was a contractor working for you and he was on a 0% deduction? You will be paying him that full money either away.

Or you say, "Well, what if we don't have the VAT money?" Well, what if you were doing some work that was VAT exempt? You wouldn't be charging that VAT amount then. Do not make the mistake of thinking that's your money from the start as it never was.

What we are trying to avoid here is if a tradesman looks into his account and sees a bank balance of 30, 40, 50 grand, whatever the amount may be. And he feels comfortable with that, but the problem is, the 50 grand might contain 20 grand of taxes. At least by following our process you will eliminate all of that.

Preliminary Tax

This is a sneaky little tax. As a sole trader in your first year it is a bit harsh to be honest, as well as paying your current income tax, the revenue wants you to pay next year's tax in advance as well!!! If there was ever a time to say " the B@$TARDS" it's when you first find out about the good aul prelim.

The prelim is calculated based on 100% of your previous year's liability or 90% of your current liability whichever is the greater.

The good thing is once you pay it once you have it done and each year you are just topping up and paying the difference between your tax bill one year and your tax bill for the following year.

After all, you should expect to be paying more tax each year as you will be earning more money year on year. Can you imagine the day when you pay €1mil in tax, that's gonna be a good one.

Corporation tax

At the time of writing this, the Corporation Tax in Ireland was set at 12.5%. This has since been slightly tweaked but the method of handling your tax in this book still applies. It is important that you keep up to date with the tax regulations as they are constantly changing. The best way to do this is by checking in with your accountant as he or she will be up to date with the most current practices around tax. Find out the rates and then apply these principles to them.

Corporation Tax, is a tax paid by limited companies but not by sole traders. The corporate tax rate in Ireland is currently 12.5% (but for how much longer we don't, know). Corporation tax is calculated on the amount of profit the company has made after all expenses, including wages and director's salaries. Any profits that are left in the company after everybody has been paid is liable for corporation tax at 12.5%.

The return date for this corporation tax will vary depending on the company's year-end but it is due 9 months and 1 day after the year-end. Corporation tax is the lowest of all the tax rates and it's not something to be greatly concerned about, because if you're paying €12,500 in corporation tax, it should mean that you are paying it out of a €100,000 that you have in your bank account.

We can talk about tax forever and when you go and talk to your accountant, he can talk to you about it forever and ever and ever. The most important thing to remember is that tax is nothing to be afraid of; if you handle it correctly from the start you won't be concerned about it.

Disclaimer:

It is important that you keep up to date with all of the tax regulations as they are constantly changing. The best way to do this is by checking in with your accountant as he or she will be up to date with the most current practices around tax. Find out the rates and then apply these principles to them.

Chapter
14

**How To Use
Your Accountant**

How to Use Your Accountant

I want to start by saying this is not an accountant bashing chapter, in fact, it is the exact opposite, I absolutely love dealing with my accountants as they are a crucial part of my business. However, you need to know how to use your accountant, and how you use your accountant will vary depending on where your business is at.

When we start in business, usually we don't know anybody else that's in business, or that has any business knowledge that can help us. As such, the only person we know is our accountant.

Accountants, by their nature, are usually very conservative people, excellent for tax compliance, excellent for tax advice and excellent for reporting. However, they are not your business mentor and they are not your business coach and don't allow yourself to fall into the bracket of using your accountant as a default business mentor or coach.

The biggest issue I see with a lot of accountants is that they should set this out for their clients from the outset, and urge their clients to go off and hire a business advisor or a business coach. But they don't. They never even bring that into play, and as such, then, the new business owner believes that the accountant is the advisor and the business coach.

The accountant has two main duties. The first duty is to report on the past performance of the company. That is, compile the year-end accounts and report back to you on how the company performed within that specific period.

So, in October of one year, they will tell you how you, as a sole trader, performed in the previous year. Or if you're a limited company, some months after your year-end, they will let you know how your company performed. This is what I mean by reporting on the past performance of the company.

The second duty of your accountant is to ensure you stay compliant with taxes. Your accountant must ensure that you stay compliant with all taxes, he should let you know filing dates and filing amounts also.

That is pretty much the two main things that you should depend on your accountant for when you're in a start-up phase. A good benchmark is when you're in a situation where you're earning less than €50,000 per year in a limited company after you've taken yourself a good, healthy, decent wage.

After €50,000 a year profit, the accountants can begin to provide strategic tax planning and help with finance applications later, but that's down the road. Right now, you need to understand they have two duties, report on the past performance of the company, and ensure compliance with taxes.

If you are thinking of launching a new product or service, the best approach is to plough on with your plans, put the wheels in motion and then revert to your accountant on what taxation treatment the new venture will get.

The biggest issue we are facing here at all times is not the amount of tax we pay, but the lack of sales which we generate and as such, we need to prioritise pushing forward with more sales all of the time.

In the same manner, if you are purchasing any assets such as vehicles, land, property, machinery you would plough on with the process. Establish the need, look at the finances and before you proceed, you would then get the accountant to throw his eye over things for you.

If I were an accountant (which I am most definitely not) and new clients were coming into me, I would tell them not to be worrying about taxes just yet and focus all of their energy on sales. I would also be advising the client to hire someone immediately to help with sales and the lead generation process. In all my years I have never heard an accountant say that to a start-up company or even a small company that has been around for a few years.

Remember this:

NEW SALES WILL FORGIVE ALL PAST MISTAKES

So, no matter what happens or has happened in the business, it is the new sales that will allow you to trade out of any bind and move forward with your business.

So whilst I'm telling you this and it seems quite easy, most business owners will never get into a situation where they can have a serious conversation about their business with somebody who is not their accountant, and who has their best interests at heart. And whilst most business owners will not do that, we also know that most businesses fail.

I think it's safe to say there would be a fairly close link between those who don't hire a business coach or a business mentor, and the businesses that fail. But at the same time, this chapter is not about business coaching or business mentorship.

This chapter is about how you use your accountant. Your accountant is there to perform two roles. The first one is to report on the past performance of the company. The second one is to ensure compliance with taxes.

I'm not telling you to go in and have it out with your accountant in any way. They perform an essential service, in fact before this book went to print I had my accountant review the tax section.

They also do things like payroll services and stuff like that as well, which I suppose forms part of ensuring compliance with taxes.

But just understand, when you're speaking with them, and they're saying things to you, or they're giving you instructions or guidance or whatever, a lot of the accountants will straddle their area of being an accountant and move towards business growth or business advice. Just be very careful.

I need to be very clear in this instance, and at the risk of repeating myself. I am advising you that as a startup or small business, your accountant is highly unlikely to give you guidance and advice on generating business or creating sales.

During the conversations with your accountant, this area of business is likely to be absent from the conversation. They may mention to you that sales are low or sales are high but they are unlikely to give you much help or guidance on generating sales other than maybe going to networking events.

Be aware of the lack of this guidance during your initial meetings and know that, in business, sales is everything. Later on, as you do more complex transactions and, in particular, property transactions, you will need to have your accountant involved throughout the process. However, for you as a startup or a business looking to drive sales, get out and get them now and the accountant will account for them later on in the books.

I like to stick to my own ethos of, only take advice from those who have done what you are trying to do. The accountants form part of the team, but an accountant is a conservative person by nature.

In the same manner, it is the duty of a good mentor who specialises in your niche to crack the whip and urge you to be pushing and driving more sales. It is the accountant's job to keep a decent rein on you and make sure you don't make any mistakes that land you in hot water later on.

Chapter 15

Mind, Body, Wallet

Mind, Body, Wallet

We are going to cover a slightly different topic now. The main philosophy of my life is Mind, Body, Wallet, in that order. I am on a mission to make €100mil and I will do whatever it takes to get to that point, however, I won't do anything immoral or illegal or anything I don't believe in, I also won't do it at the expense of my mental health, my physical health or at the expense of my family. Other than that, I will go all in, but it has to be in that order.

Many tradesmen and self-employed people neglect both their physical and mental health while growing their business and I strongly urge you not to do the same.

Let's talk first about the Mind. I don't in any way class myself as an expert on this topic so what I am sharing with you is my own point of view. A lot of this has been shaped by the teachings I have received from Grant Cardone who is a hero of mine, and I strongly urge you to follow him online. He's one cool operator, so Grant, thank you for helping turn me into the beast that I am today. See you at the top, my friend.

Mind

The first thing you must do is control your environment; you cannot physically control how every single thing is in your environment, but you can control if you are in that environment or not. More often than not I leave WhatsApp groups, I leave Facebook groups, I leave physical rooms and physical conversations because the topics being discussed are purely polluting my mind.

We need to be very careful about the type of conversations we allow ourselves to hear either passively or actively. I don't engage in chit-chat or backchat and I don't hang around to listen to it myself either.

The quality of our life depends greatly on the quality of the conversations we have with the people in our life, and this is the most important thing to take on board. I have been threatening to write this book for over 1 year now before starting, and I kept putting it on the long finger. About 6 weeks ago I was on the 6 o'clock news when my friend and award-winning book writer Pat Falvey called me to say well done. During the conversation I mentioned I was going to write a book and he wouldn't let me get off the phone until I told him when it would be done.

Pat is a well-known adventurer, has climbed Everest more than once and has been to the south pole countless times. He's a real-life adventurer and has written several books about his travels. So he knows his stuff when it comes to writing books. Anyways, I told Pat I would have the book written while I was on my holidays as I was going to Spain for a month. In the end, I never got to write the book within the month so when I flew back to Ireland I left the very next day to get back to write this book.

I believe the reason I didn't get to write the book within the first month is that the environment I was in wasn't very inspiring. I had rented a nice house in the centre of town for myself and my family to live in, but there was too much concrete and not enough nature.

Now I am in a nice spacious villa in the mountains. In the garden, there is a lemon tree, a grapevine, an olive tree and a fig tree and lots of space. For me at least, this is an inspiring environment. So, it is important to control both your physical environment and the emotional environment.

Not all of us have the resources to lock ourselves away in a villa in the mountains for a month so I get that 100%. However, all of us have the resources to lock out negative BS that isn't going to serve us well at all.

If you want to be successful you must eliminate where possible or, at the very least reduce, the contact time as much as possible with anyone - be they a stranger, a client, a staff member, a supplier, a contractor or even a family member - who has a bad attitude. If you're trying to operate at a new higher level, you must eliminate this type of energy as much as possible as it will drag you down. You would not allow someone to come into your house and empty their wheelie bin all over your floor and then walk out of your house leaving all the rubbish behind, so why would you allow someone to treat your headspace like that.

Once you have all the BS eliminated, it is then down to you to fill your head with good stuff, focus only on the good, practice being grateful and practice being happy.

To access any Downloads mentioned in this book go to:
www.joedoyle.ie/tsgfreeresources

Body

Once we have the head in a good place we must keep it there. For me, I train regularly and won't miss training purely for work. For a long time, the only legitimate reason I would accept for missing training was that I was working. Work got priority over training every day of the week. I would usually train in the evening after work, however, if I was working late I would give it a miss. Then I hired a personal trainer to keep me accountable and booked my training schedule into the diary like any other business meeting.

Once I put it in the diary I just made it happen.

I also watch what I eat. Nowadays I eat a 99% plant based diet. I don't eat meat and I feel the benefit of it every day. The reason I say 99% is because 1 day someone will see me eating some non-plant based food and be only more than happy to call me out on it. I am 100% determined, 100% motivated, 100% entrepreneur and only 99% plant eater. Occasionally I do a 24-hour fast but every day I normally fast for 17 hours. I start every morning with a two-minute cold shower and when I get out I feel like I can take over the world.

I am by no means saying you need to do all of these things if you want to be successful in your business, but people regularly ask me how I manage to get so much done and I put it down in some way to the combination of choices I make to look after my mindset and my body.

To access any Downloads mentioned in this book go to:
www.joedoyle.ie/tsgfreeresources

My advice would be that you at least try and figure out what works for you. And I would start with reducing your meat intake, and maybe try a weekend without eating meat or any animal based products and see how you feel after that.

Wallet

Notice how the wallet is the last of the three, get the mind and body taken care of. Now we can focus entirely on the wallet. To quote the words of Grant Cardone, *'Success is your duty, obligation and responsibility.'* It is not just an optional extra that we will add in at the end if everything goes well for us.

The day I started treating success as my duty, is the day things took a step up for me. I have a duty to be a good partner, a good son, a good father, a good friend, a good employer and I also have a duty to be successful. I don't differentiate between them all.

I once put a Facebook post out asking what name would you use to describe someone who could afford to pay for life-saving treatment for a loved one but simply wouldn't?

The post went crazy with people writing all sorts of less than flattering names in the comments.

I then followed up with a post asking what name would you use to describe someone who knew that one day they would need to have money to pay for life-saving treatment for a loved one but simply wouldn't put in the effort now?

For me I see no difference, we need to put the effort in now to become successful to create financial security and a future for all of our families. There is a lot of wealth out there in the world, you may as well go after your piece.

According to the central statistics office, there are 2,003,645 houses in Ireland. You may as well go out there and try to own a few of them as someone needs to own them and you strike me as someone who is well capable of making that happen.

If you owned just 4 houses plus your own family home that will give you a very good quality of life. The way to work towards it is by getting your €500 a day as many days as possible.

Even as I write this now I can feel myself getting fired up to go at it. I see myself as no different from a high-performance athlete, we need to be focused, we need to eat healthily, we need to train regularly.

I tell people I am an athlete in the sport of wealth creation, and I urge you to become one too. And if you do, when you truly make the commitment and you truly treat success as your duty, you will soon realise that it's much easier than you believe and there are not many other people on the same path.

Chapter 16

Understanding The Numbers

Understanding The Numbers In Your Business

If you are like me, you won't be naturally very good at Excel, looking at reports and balance sheets and all that carry-on. If you're like me, you will have been going in and out of your accountants' office over the last few years on the regular when it comes to the tax time of year, and he will tell you how much you have made and unfortunately in some cases, how much you lost.

For a long time, I found this quite confusing as I never really knew where I stood any time he told me how much money I was making, I would always ask a simple question – *'Well, where it is because it's not in the bank account?'*. He would explain to me that it was owed in and when I collect it, I will see it in the bank account. The only problem was that I needed to spend it as it was coming in to fund further jobs, so I never really knew where I stood with it and I never had it in my hand.

The accountant would give you his opinion on whether he thought you were doing good or not. In a lot of instances, my accountant was happy to tell me how well he thought I was doing, but I wasn't as happy with my company's performance as he was. I felt I should be doing a lot better.

So, I came up with a little exercise that you can do and it will show you how good your company really is doing in the space of a couple of minutes. The beauty about this exercise is that it is not based on opinion or how you feel at the time, it is based on an absolute fact. What it does is allow you to determine the cash growth value of the business on a yearly basis. It will show how much the cash value of the business is increasing by year on year.

If you want to make a million euro and the annual cash growth of the business is €50,000 well then it's going to take you 20 years to get to your million. If you're happy with 20 years, great, stay as you are, but if 20 years is too long, then something has got to change.

Cash Value Of Business Exercise:

Grab a piece of paper and work this out:

1. Write down how many years you are in business.
2. Write down your company bank balance as it stands today.
3. Add to this amount any money that is owed in.
4. Add to this amount the value of any stock or vans or assets the company has.
5. Now from this number deduct any money you owe out.

You will now have the total cash value of your business.

The last step is to divide the total cash value of your business by the number of years you are in business.

So, if you have €50,000 as the cash value amount of your business and you are in business 10 years the annual cash growth of your business is €5,000 If you have €50,000 as the cash value amount of your business and you are in business for 2 years, the annual cash growth of your business is €25,000. In this instance, you can see the story behind the numbers, and this can completely change the perspective. Many people are only happy to beat their chest when looking at their bank balance, but when you ask them to explain how long it took them to get there and divide their bank balance by the number of years, that shows a different story altogether.

If, as you are reading this, you're adding your own numbers up in your head, you're probably thinking to yourself, well I would have had more money if I didn't buy the van or I didn't buy the tools. You can't think like that because the items that you bought for the business, you only bought for the business so that it could conduct it's business and trade.

Nobody truly wants to be driving around in a big van, we only want to be driving around in the van because it is good for work. If you were in another line of work you would not need or want the van and if you were in another line of work you would not need or want the tools. These items that you have purchased to allow your business to carry out its trading activities cannot be seen as profit. This all goes back to €500 per day which will equate to €10,000 per month which will equate to €120,000 in the bank at the end of the year, and €10,000 per month is based on working only 20 days in the month, which I know we all do a lot more than that.

You may recall earlier on when I mentioned that the danger is never in setting the bar too high and failing, the real danger is in setting the bar too low and succeeding. Many business owners are falling victim to this all of the time.

They have set the bar far too low and they are succeeding at it which is not good because they don't realise how close they are to being able to achieve something really significant in their business and their life.

When I start working with clients, I realise that it is very much an inside job, I know what they are capable of, but they don't yet believe it. So, what I do is get them to make €500 per day for 20 days.

We set some targets and objectives and we make sure they make their clear profit of €10,000 in the month. Sometimes it takes a number of months to help them get to it, but they usually get there eventually.

After that, we then find out what was the most amount of cash they ever had in their bank account. After all, if they had that level of cash in the past, surely they can do it again. We aren't asking them to do anything that they have not done before. It is about increasing their level of self-belief.

It is about increasing their earning capacity in layers because every time we go up a level, we need to become a different version of ourselves. It requires a different skillset to do a lot, than it does to get a lot done. Many tradesmen are very guilty of telling a lad to leave a task that he will do himself rather than spending the time to show the lad how to do it himself. It is this way of thinking that will keep people trapped where they are and not allow them to move on.

I'm a firm believer that the universe will give you what you want, you only need to ask for it. That is why we need to set out early on with a purpose for our business and that is why I always recommend the purpose being a daily numerical amount because at the end of the day, you can determine on a yes or no basis if the business has achieved its purpose for that day.

If you were to set the purpose of your business to reach and help people, or to make you happy, that's great, but it is a bit wishy-washy and there is no way of knowing if you are winning or not, as you will base your opinion of your business on how you are feeling emotionally at that time. We want to take emotion out of the equation. You need the answer to be given to you like the flick of a switch. It is either yes, or no.

Just remember €500 a day, €500 a day, €500 a day.

Chapter
17

Getting To €500 A Day

Getting To €500 A Day

I get contacted by people all the time who tell me they want to be property investors and property developers, or that they are business owners and they want to buy a couple of properties which is all good in my eyes. So when someone tells me of their big plans that may take months or years to achieve and they want me to help them out with that, the first thing I do is make a small plan and see how willing they are to stick with it and to see how they handle a challenge.

"So, you want to be a millionaire, right?", I say. "Do you have what it takes, can you keep focused?"

They usually answer yes, to which I then say "Ok. Let's figure out how we can make a €500 clear profit in the next 24 hours". Actually, I would recommend you try this exercise yourself.

If you have no work on, let's commit to making €500 profit by close of business tomorrow. If you are already busy and have work on, let's commit to making an extra €500 profit by close of business tomorrow. The trick about the €500 challenge is that it is usually out of reach, but only slightly out of reach. Just imagine you trying to get something off a top-shelf that you can only just barely grab once you stretch and jump. If the target is too high you won't go after it, if the target is too low, well then what's the point of that.

Going after a target that is just barely out of your reach is a good way to grow as it doesn't take long for this target to become your new-normal, after which we can increase the target again and then repeat the process.

I hold a firm belief that any tradesman can make €500 in a day, in this day and age. As I mentioned before, the difficulty is being able to do it consistently. Now before you start having a canary saying "You won't get €500 a day in my area" or "My trade sure the day rate is only XX and if I go into a lad and tell him '*I want €500 a day*' he's going to tell me to get lost". Here is how you do it.

- Firstly never tell any client or employer that you want to make €500 a day

- Stop working for an hourly rate, stop quoting people on a day rate and stop comparing yourself to others who are already operating like this.

You must now figure out a way to offer a service to your clients where you don't charge per hour anymore. You need to sell the value that you deliver, don't just sell your time.

Chris O Conor - Elite Woodworking Machinery:

When I started working with my client Chris O Connor of Elite Woodworking Machinery, he was struggling to hit his daily targets and then we analysed his processes.

The issue we had was that he was charging per hour, but he had so much downtime between jobs that he could not bill a full 8 hours per day. The thing with Chris is he is a top-class operator and prides himself on the service he gives his clients. He knows that if his clients call him for a breakdown it is because their machine has stopped working and they are now losing money, so he's only too willing to drop everything and run to them.

We were exploring either increasing the hourly rate right across the board or putting them on a pricing system rather than an hourly rate. It turned out the pricing system wasn't viable and Chris didn't want to increase his hourly rate across the board as he is happy with the rate his clients were paying when the jobs he goes to run on for 4 hours or more.

After giving it some thought, it turned out that the best way Chris's business could achieve its purpose and hit its targets was for Chris to simply put a 2-hour minimum charge for each call out. If the job took an hour, they pay for two hours, if the job took two hours, they pay for two hours. Generally speaking, the clients don't mind paying the minimum call-out charge as he's always at the end of the phone. This then gave Chris the ability to try and tie in his non-emergency scheduled work with the locations where the emergency works normally came from. So, in a lot of instances, he is never far away. This only increases the value to the client even more. The 2-hour minimum call-out fee, plus the fact that Chris can be on- site within 30 minutes works very well for Chris's clients as when their machines stop working they are losing money.

The above example is just one way we can increase our productivity and profitability whilst delivering a better service to our clients. One of the biggest game-changers I had with a client while trying to get them to embrace the €500 a day target was with a client called Gary Martin of OCM in Offaly.

Gary Martin - OCM:

Gary started with us and I was reviewing his pipeline of work. We identified a number of items of work that were simply never going to allow him hit his target. Gary is a very determined operator and if he gives you his word that he will do something he most definitely will. When I saw that he needed to drop a certain type of work from his list of services his mind immediately went to, *'What would the clients say?'*, and he felt like he was letting them down. While Gary was thinking that by not doing this work he was letting the clients down, I was of the opinion, that by him doing these types of jobs, the only people he was letting down was himself and his young son Oisin.

Gary and I are chatting away, and I was getting some resistance from him. As a business mentor, my job is to show my clients a better way, especially when they cannot see that way at that time. Rather than push more and more, I asked Gary if he would be willing to have this conversation online with my other clients in the audience to offer feedback.

The reason for this is because if he is struggling to believe me, he will be more willing to believe me when there are 30 or 40 other people I have also gone through the same process with previously listening in and giving their feedback. In fairness to Gary, he agreed, and you could hear the uncomfortableness in his voice but when all of the other lads started giving him encouragement he agreed to go along with it.

The next day he went and told some of his clients that he can't do certain jobs, in particular one client with whom he was due to start a big job for the following week. Gary texted me later the following day to say he had just had one of the most difficult conversations he ever had to have but he knows it was the right thing. Since then, Gary's business has been going from strength to strength and it is a pleasure to have him as a client. We recorded that particular conversation between myself and Gary with the feedback from the other community members and we now use it as a case study for when other tradesmen are uncomfortable making decisions that they know are the right decision to make but they are having difficulty with it.

When your business is going to make a profit, it can usually only come from one of three areas.

1. The profit on selling your own labour

2. The profit on selling the labour of your staff

3. The profit you make on the materials you provide.

Sometimes it is easy to work out which of these areas you are making your profit on. If you are selling a completed extension or say, an item of furniture, it will be difficult to pinpoint if you are making the profit on the materials or the labour as you are now selling the unit, but either way that's where the profit is coming from.

Now that we are aiming for €500 per day we need to split out where this money is coming from: if you have two staff plus yourself and you supply materials, it can be quite easy. Say €100 margin on the materials and €133 profit per man per day.

If you are thinking €500 per day is too much, I'm sure once we break it down for you to €133 profit per day per man it may seem more achievable. Way back when I started out as a business mentor, I was pushing my clients for €10,000 profit a month. The reason why I started with €10,000 per month is because that was what my target was when I started out in business. I got a lot of resistance when trying to encourage men to aim for €10,000 per month. But when I changed this to €500 a day it then appeared more achievable to them. And when we divide €10,000 by €500 a day it gives us 20 days.

I don't believe there is any self-employed tradesman in the country that works only 20 days per month. When you think of it, €500 a day is a lot more than €10,000 per month, yet €500 a day is more achievable in their eyes and to be honest that's all that matters.

When you start aiming for €500 a day you will need to audit your pipeline of work by carrying out a past job analysis. If you do work that takes a number of days, the magic number to be watching out for here is the profit per job per day. Numbers on a page only show numbers on a page, they don't show the grief and timescale behind getting to that number and that's why we must break it down even further to a per-day basis and even note which one of your staff is producing the higher profits consistently.

After completing this exercise, it is most likely that you will see the higher profits coming from certain jobs or works carried out by certain staff members. If you would like a template to carry out the past job analysis, go to www. joedoyle.ie/tsgfreeresources and check out the Past Job Analysis Template.

When you then figure out what your most profitable works are, you need to become a specialist in that type of work. The more of a specialist you can become in that area the more likely you are to stand out. Say for example you are a general builder, I might be Joe Doyle General Building Contractors, a specialist in 'Wet Room Extensions'

This is a lot better than Joe Doyle General Building Contractors, all types of works undertaken.

We still can undertake all types of works but when you specialise in something people will remember you.

My building company was called InsuranceWorks.ie; we specialised in 'Insurance Based Property Repairs' and we ruled the roost when it came to that type of work in our location. Nobody could compete with us because we were the specialists and everything about us screamed specialist.

Some years ago, when I started doing work on social media and helping people with their businesses, I was willing to help anyone with anything as I am naturally a good problem solver.

Then I started to follow my own advice, I saw who I was having the most success with and I niched down. Today I am happy to say I am the number 1 business mentor in Ireland for tradesmen and the construction industry. If you check out my bio on my Facebook page it says:

Showing TRADESMEN a clear path to €500 profit per day & opening their eyes to property investment.

When it comes to what I do, nobody can compete with me because although I am a specialist, I am also a product of my own philosophy. On the back of following my systems, I have created a net worth in the millions and a property company with a valuation of more than €12 million (and counting). Eventually, one day, a competitor will come along to try to knock me off the number one spot, but in order to do so he must be topping what I have managed to achieve by following my own practices and systems, otherwise they will just be another guy who learned something from a book.

Anyways back to helping you become a specialist, don't just be Joe Bloggs Plumber or Joe Bloggs Carpentry.

Try becoming a specialist in your location and your industry. When I started working with Andy Ward, he was Andrew Ward Window Repairs. After working together for a bit, we decided it was best if he became 'The Window Repair Company' simply as that stronger sounding name. It's as if he has been around forever. Andy had a business before which failed and then he went back to employment for a couple of years and got his mortgage but he knew he wanted to be a business owner, so the second time around he hired me to help him out and although it's still early days, he has been doing extremely well ever since.

If you have a particularly bad sore throat and you pay the doctor €50 to go in and get a prescription, he may suggest you need to see a specialist and give you a referral letter. You then go and see the specialist who will charge you €200 for pretty much the same job as the doctor has done. He may tell you to take the medication and call him back if it gets worse.

The moral of the story here is that the specialist will always earn more, and you will be more than happy to pay more to see the specialist purely because he is the specialist so keep that in mind.

Chapter 18

How To Find Good Staff

How To Find Good Staff

At the time of writing, one of the biggest challenges facing small employers in the construction space is the lack of manpower.

Unfortunately, right now it is an employee's market. When I say unfortunately I mean that for both the employer and the economy. At all times it should be an employer's market where potential employees know that they need to be on their A-game to get and hold down a job, whereas nowadays they know they can walk in and out of jobs. The big multinational companies are offering packages that are so cushy people are willing to take them. I feel a bit of pity for guys who are working in big multinational companies as they are shielded from the reality of the daily grind so if they ever find themselves back in our world, which I class as the real world, they will definitely be in for a rude awakening.

I remember a friend who works as a contractor for a multinational telling me a story about how they have a 24-hour emergency line to contact one of the main men in the event of a big emergency. One of the staff made a call in the small hours of the morning kicking up an absolute stink because he had asked for a new pair of work boots and didn't get them yet. I know what sort of boot I would have been giving him if he had that attitude with me.

Either way, this is the way, this is how it is for now, so we need to be able to come up with a solution to deal with it. I don't want to say this, but the reality is one day the economy will turn and only the strong will survive and all these slackers will be struggling to find work and blaming it on everyone else.

The best way I have found to attract new staff is to make your company a good place to work. I have zero issues finding new staff ever, but I believe this is because of my position in the public eye. Every week I get people reaching out saying they want to work with me, but my company is different. We are the only property company or tradesmen mentorship company that is really publicly pushing our brand on social media but I know it wouldn't be the same if I was running a traditional construction company.

The truth be told, when it comes to hiring people our biggest concern is we get stuck with some tool of a chap that becomes more of a hindrance to the business than a help. What I find very effective is if we can come up with a watertight process to get rid of him before we even hire him. Let's be honest, it is a bit uncomfortable when we have to let someone go.

After the discomfort of having to let someone go, the next biggest issue we as business owners allow ourselves to get caught out by is that we wait until we absolutely 100% need someone before we start looking. When we start looking we want to find the perfect person first time around and because we are so busy we don't have the time necessary to put into finding the right person, so what happens here is we take on the first person that comes along and, during the interview, rather than looking objectively to see if the person is the right fit, we try to find aspects of their profile and imagine that they will do the job, but they, unfortunately, won't and it doesn't take long before that becomes apparent.

Think of it this way, let's say you meet some chick, (or a dude if that's how you roll) on tinder or a dating app and when you rock up to the first date she is sitting there in a wedding dress. She turns around and says I liked your profile so I thought you might be good marriage material, so I decided we should get married. Of course you would run a mile because there's a good chance you could come home within a few weeks to see your pet rabbit being cooked in the kitchen. I know this is a crazy extreme example, but this is what you're doing when it comes to hiring people. You are that crazy chick in the wedding dress on the first date. You are looking to get perfect hires first time around and it rarely works. So, here's two strategies that I want you to use going forward.

Rolling Recruitment Policy

Your company must have a rolling recruitment policy and what that means is you must be willing to take on someone new every week for at least one day's work. Be sure to put it out there all the time that you are always looking for new staff, of any description.

Eventually, when you get a call from someone who is looking for work as either a carpenter, a plumber, a sparks, whatever the trade happens to be, tell them that you have a big job due to start in a couple of weeks and you should be able to find them a couple of days' work here and there between now and then, would that suit them?

If They Say NO:

If they say no because they absolutely want something steady and would rather sit at home and collect the scratcher than go and work for the same money. Well in my opinion you don't want them anyways.

If They Say YES:

If they say yes just give them a shout, the next thing you should say to them is, I may not have a bit of trades work but there will definitely be a bit of labouring work while we are waiting on the bigger job to start, would this suit you?

If they do not say to you something along the lines of an absolute YES, well then you don't want them on your team either way. I have always found that the guy who can get €250 or so off the scratcher per week for sitting at home while he is out of work and the other guy would rather work a couple of days in the week and still only get €250, these guys are worlds apart in terms of their attitude.

In the same way as the guy who says I'm a carpenter, I didn't serve my time as a carpenter only to go labouring for brickie's or plasterers. He is usually worlds apart from the carpenter who says, I don't mind, work is work. It's better than sitting in the house and it's only until the big job starts.

To access any Downloads mentioned in this book go to:
www.joedoyle.ie/tsgfreeresources

During the call you are looking for the guy who has the YES, I CAN attitude. The difference between the way you are doing this now, and the way you were doing it before is that if you start early enough, you won't be stuck for the lads, you won't need him to start right away. What we are doing here is looking for some diamonds in the rough because if they impress you, you will definitely find a permanent placement for them.

Right now, because you are only opening your eyes up to this way of sourcing staff, you may be stuck for someone. But you still need to go about it in the same way, even if your life is depending on this guy to start right away. Tell him you have a big job starting in a couple of weeks but sure if he wants to come down tomorrow you could do with a lad for the day. If at the end of the day he looks like he's worth a shot, ask him to call in the next day.

If he performs the second day ask him if he is ok for the week. If he's ok for the week ask him if he is ok for a full week next week. By the end of the second week, you will know if this guy is a team player and then you can employ him and put him on probation. If you don't feel like he's a team player you don't need to tell him you think he's no good, you can tell him the other job got put back for a few weeks, or it's starting as scheduled but the works got scaled back and you will give him a call when the job gets rolling properly.

If you think back to the earlier chapter where I mentioned that you don't need to make somebody wrong just so you can be right, that's exactly what we are doing here. You don't need to make this guy wrong just so you can be right.

What we need to bear in mind here is, our industry is quite small and we will be operating with a small pool of people, and tradesmen regularly move around the different employers but, most importantly, they all talk and you always want people talking positively about you. It is always worthwhile to have this rolling recruitment policy going on.

There should be one new guy every week doing at least one day's work with you. If you don't have this going on you will definitely run into staffing issues at some point in the future. We want to start now so we have this tackled before it becomes an issue.

People want to do business with winners

If there's one thing that's true in every walk of life it's that people want to hang out with and do business with winners. Nobody wants to hang out with a loser, so if you're looking to attract new staff, your business must be seen as a winning place to work at. A strategy that is worthwhile to use is to use your ads as space not only to tell people to buy your stuff but to showcase your work and that you are expanding and you are looking to hire more people.

Here's an example of a mistake I see business owners making all the time. Take for example a kitchen fitting company and they run ads online showing the latest kitchen they have just completed and it says something along the lines of *'this could be yours for €10,000'* or *'contact us if you want a quote for a kitchen.'*

That's all fine, there is nothing wrong with that. However, when they are then looking to hire someone they post an ad on a completely different platform like one of the job-seeking sites, which again is fine or they post an ad in the same location where they were posting their work ads. Only this time when they are posting the vacancy ad, they include a picture that says WE ARE HIRING!!!

I always recommend that you keep posting the same type of images in your ads, which is the images of your work. If you put some decent text in the ad to say that you are looking to hire a top-quality tradesman whilst still showcasing your work, it means you are getting a double whammy on the ad.

The potential client is looking and saying well if they are hiring they must be a good company. This will then give them surety and help remove any doubts they have about approaching your company.

The potential client may also know someone who is looking for a job in which case they will be happy to refer you.

If you post the ad saying WE ARE HIRING!!! this will not appeal to most of the usual audience that you have built up. Keep showcasing your work and keep mentioning that you are hiring. Below I will give you an example of Ad text that you can use to find staff for your business.

Job ad text example you can use to find new staff:

'ABC Kitchen company is delighted to say we are looking to expand our team of 4 kitchen fitters to 5. If you know anyone who would like to work with one of the most well- respected kitchen companies around, please do get in touch. We are happy to say we can still take enquiries from new clients but are seeking to expand our team. For information on the kitchen featured below, please contact the page.'

Chapter 19

_____

For Those Running
Bigger Companies

For those running bigger companies

If you're running a company that turns over more than €2million per year this chapter is specifically for you. Every other chapter has been written based on my own experience in the building industry where I ran a building company for 10 years that was turning around €1mil each year, most years it was just below the 7 figures.

This chapter is different as the information in this chapter is based on what I have learned about €2mil+ companies since I left the construction industry and since I commenced works in the business mentorship space.

The one thing that we all need to agree on from the outset is the amount of profit we make should be in direct proportion to the following: the amount of work we do, the amount of risk we take and the amount of capital we outlay.

We also need to agree that it is not about doing work for work's sake, it is purely about making profits. The ideal job, as we mentioned earlier in the book, is the job where you can get 1 day's work, for one man and on the back of that get one year's profit, while at the same time as collecting payment, the client books you in for the same job next year. As we know it is unlikely (never say impossible) we can get this type of job, so we have to get as close as possible to this type of job and we scale back to the point where we can get 1 and a half days wages per man for every day we have 1 man on a job.

So while I have many lads who passed through my program, albeit smaller operators and on the tools on a full time or even part-time basis who are turning over 350k but making 100k profit after a salary of 50k. we have bigger company's turning over €2mil. The director may be taking a 100k salary and the company makes 100k profit. This means that the bigger company is making 50k profit extra per year, however, the chance of any of the following happening is huge for the €2mil+ company.

1. Getting sued by clients
2. Getting sued by staff
3. Not getting paid by clients
4. Contracts being cancelled
5. Not getting retention amount
6. Suppliers going bust.

These items are an issue for any business regardless of size, however the bigger the company the greater the risk of this happening. Once you start going into bigger numbers, you need an entirely new layer of staff and management which then eats up massive costs. Your gross margin remains decent, but your net margin becomes razor-thin due to the extra overhead.

In a lot of instances, I have struggled to get lasting results with these types of businesses as I have struggled to get the owners of the companies to follow my guidance. After all, why should they listen to me (even after they have hired me) they are turning 2mil, 3mil + a year, they have 20+ people under them, why should they listen to a former bricklayer who is usually 10 and sometimes 20 years younger than them.

Either way, massive respect to them for what they have done so far, but the thinking that got them there is also the same thinking that will hold them back from getting to the next level and unfortunately this profile of business owner is usually either stuck in their ways or very focused, but it is not the profits they are focused on it is the turnover and the running of a big company.

When I start dealing with a client at this level I normally employ a strategy where we discuss the number of times in the past that the business has 'almost' run out of cash and the company owner went off and pulled a rabbit out of a hat and made everything ok again.

Normally a company of this size will have had plenty of scenarios in the past where things got tight for them, but they managed to pull through. After we have identified that things got tight many times, but they lived to tell the tale, we are usually then in agreement that they are good at saving the company in times of difficulty. The next step is then to get the company owner to agree to set aside €1,000 in a separate account every week. This money is just set aside but not taken out of the company, after 6 months we look at increasing this amount of money, setting it aside, but again not taking it out of the company.

After 12 months it is then agreed that the company will not need this money, but it has been saved and it could have been saved all along had the company owner just had the discipline to do it. It will also be agreed that the company hasn't missed this money, it didn't feel like it was left short in any way.

Martin Dormer - Hollyfort Services

One company that we had success with using this strategy is Hollyfort Services. Hollyfort is a big company that is well respected in the industry, turning over several million per year and with a lot of high-end contracts. Martin Dormer is the main man here, an absolute gentleman and as sharp as a tack. When I first started working with Martin it was more out of curiosity for him. The company was doing well. They weren't short on sales or cash and things were in a good place. Martin just has a natural hunger for growth and improvement so when he connected with me I felt we were a good fit. As Hollyfort was being run so well, it wasn't for me to get involved and start tinkering too much, but rather make the suggestion that we hire the **'phantom employee'**.

We set aside 1 wage every week as if it was due to be paid out to another employee. No sooner was this up and running than it became the new normal within the business and after a few months it was increased and I believe at time of writing it has been increased a number of times.

This simple strategy is overlooked all the time and the sooner you start to implement it the better. At the end of the first year, over the Christmas holiday, I got a WhatsApp from Martin to tell me how much he had managed to accumulate since implementing the strategy. I asked him how he felt about it and he sent me a very brief message:

"Should have done it a long time ago.."

After we have some success with our phantom employee strategy, I always advise that we now take this money and we use it to buy a property, either via a company or personally, there are slight differences between each strategy and each with their pro's and con's but that's a conversation for another time.

The reason why I insist on this strategy is purely down to my belief that you should always use your business as a vehicle for wealth creation; you must always, from day one, be taking some money off the table and out of the business, and the reason for this is purely down to the fact that most businesses do not stand the test of time and this is not in any way a comment on the owners of the businesses who we are referring to here. It is purely a fact that most businesses do not stand the test of time.

Use your business as a vehicle for wealth creation, use your business to buy cash-generating assets that you can use to replace your income as time goes on.

Bert Galbraith - Galbraith Construction

Bert Galbraith runs Galbraith Construction in Donegal. They do a lot of work for the council and most likely they are the best-known operator in their area. It took me quite a while to get Bert on to my program as he didn't specifically need to be there as business was going well for him and Bert definitely knows his stuff.

Anyways, one day myself and Bert got on the phone and we had a chat with the outcome being, sure we will try it for a month and see how we get on. The biggest benefit that I could offer Bert was mostly in the line of using the business as the vehicle for wealth creation and just trying to squeeze a little bit more out of the company. Bert called me up one day out of the blue to ask if I would know anyone or would I be interested in buying a particular property in his area.

We spent a few minutes chatting away when I mentioned to him that he should buy it. He was having a particularly busy time in the business and he should use the fruits of this busy time in his business to buy a property. I explained that he needs to be able to look back and be able to say, my reward for working so hard during this period is that I now own XX address.

Also, just because he didn't have the money right now, doesn't mean he can't get the money to buy the property. We discussed a number of strategies that would allow Bert to utilise the resources that he had in order to buy the property, that set off a spark in his head and he was all over it like a rash.

Bert didn't do that exact deal which I think was a good call, but he sent me a WhatsApp a few weeks later of the house he did buy, which is better suited to him.

Of course, Bert & Martin don't need me on their team. They are knocking it out of the park themselves already, but having an open mind and, most importantly, by allowing themselves to take on board a different perspective, it has improved their companies and it will continue to do so.

Flicking back to my earlier point where I have mentioned that, up until now, I sometimes struggle to get the owners of these companies to follow my program. I have since analysed the data obtained during these interactions and the only reasoning that I can come up with is one of the following:

5 Reasons Why I Find It Difficult To Get Results with Bigger Companies:

1. Either they do not take me seriously because I have personally never run a company turning over that level of sales every year and I am always proud to say, I will only talk about topics & experiences that I have been through and experienced myself; although I have made multiples of the profit they are currently making – I had to get that one in there.

2. Getting change into such a big company is hard because of the number of different people and layers of staff, to which the owner is simply not willing to put the effort in to.

3. The company owner has never experienced a liquidation or bankruptcy and as such, they are oblivious to the risks they are taking, whereas I have experienced both liquidation and a bankruptcy (almost) and as such, I now see the value of the concept of using your company 'as a vehicle for wealth creation'.

4. The company owners do not know or believe there is a better, easier way of doing things. My niche is tradesmen and small builders who are at the start-up stage up to €1mil per year. We can help these guys get significant results in their businesses in a relatively short space of time. Following the processes in this book, it is possible to get to the point where I can get a guy on the path to making 120k per year with himself and 3 staff so if you are running a bigger company just contrast your results towards these results and make sure you are getting well rewarded for the risk you are taking.

5. The company owners are simply too proud to take instructions because they have 'built this company up from scratch' and they don't need anyone telling them how they should do things.

Let's say you are running a €2mil+ company, and you want to get more profitable, what advice would I have for you? The first one is, starting today, you should set aside €1,000 per week as mentioned earlier. The second thing I would highly recommend is that you add a new service that is similar to what you are doing but you can get paid in advance or immediately upon completion and take no longer than 1 day to complete. Normally this is something along the lines of a service or maintenance contract. We want to avoid any 30-days to get paid type of job and we want to avoid any jobs that will take an extended period of time. Ideally, it is a service where you can get paid via credit card.

Effectively, you want to set up a micro company within your company. If you do this correctly you can use the staff to deliver this service on dead time where you have them doing filler work or just giving other lads a hand.

I know for sure if we audited the day of all of your staff, you would find that there would be an amount of leakage in there and they are not spending all of their time on IGTs.

By sending staff to do other smaller jobs, particularly if this is a new service, sometimes you can get a bit of resistance from them and the best thing to do is allocate one person to this new service and you send him to help out on the main jobs when there is slack on the new service. Do not hire any new staff for this exercise; it must come from within your current pool of manpower.

The question that you need to go off now and find the answer to is:

What can I possibly do to generate more sales from within my existing business without hiring more staff?

If you are like Martin or Bert who we mentioned above, and you want to take things up a notch on the property side of things, maybe you should connect with me so we can help you formulate a plan.

Chapter 20

The Make Or Break Operating System

The Make Or Break Operating System

Up until now, most of the items covered in the book have been single tactics that you can deploy at various crossroads in your business.

Now we are going to talk about an overall strategy. Sometimes people don't understand the difference between tactics and strategy, but let me explain it to you with a little help from a thing called Google:

"Strategy is overarching plan or set of goals. Tactics are the specific actions or steps you undertake to accomplish your strategy."

My MAKE-OR-BREAK operating system is a complete strategy and operating system for any small business. When you turn on a laptop, regardless of the make of the laptop, usually what you see on screen is Microsoft Windows. This is the operating system for the laptop and without it there is not a lot the laptop can do.

For small construction businesses, the biggest issue is usually the complete lack of an operating system that's tailored for the business, but fear no more: after this chapter you will have a complete operating system and you will be able to achieve the mission of the business and hit your target of €500 per day or whatever multiple of €500 per day you are aiming for. So, let's dive right in.

The MAKE-OR-BREAK operating system comprises of 9 parts, and they must all be followed in a specific order. Even as I write this paragraph, I know in the future I will get queries from people who tell me they glanced over a part of the system because they felt they didn't need it, but I will have to say I told you so when you fall short on the overall goal by not following each part.

Part 1: Set The Mission Of The Business

The mission of the business is to make a clear and absolute profit of €500 per day, or multiples of €500 per day, so that we can purchase some cash producing investments so we can take care of our family financially - full stop.

End of mission statement of business. Notice that our mission statement is **not:**

To make a clear and absolute profit of €500 per day or multiples of €500 per day, providing the economy doesn't tank.

Notice that our mission statement is **not:**

To make a clear and absolute profit of €500 per day or multiples of €500 per day, providing no key staff leave the business.

Notice that our mission statement is **not:**

To make a clear and absolute profit of €500 per day or multiples of €500 per day, providing nobody tries to rip us off.

Notice that our mission statement is **not:**

To make a clear and absolute profit of €500 per day or multiples of €500 per day, providing the banks will give us finance.

Notice that our mission statement is **not:**

To make a clear and absolute profit of €500 per day or multiples of €500 per day, providing we are successful at winning tenders.

Notice that our mission statement is **not:**

To make a clear and absolute profit of €500 per day or multiples of €500 per day, providing the business doesn't interfere with my football training.

We could make this list as long as we want, but I'm sure by now you get my point. The mission is the mission, end of story. I have said this many, many times. All that we need to be in life and in business is the type of person who does what they say they are going to do.

We've set the mission, and that's it. We are now going to hit our target of €500 clear and absolute profit per day.

Part 2: Eliminate All Distractions

If you have more than 1 business running, and yet neither of them is making you a clear and absolute profit of €500 per day, I can tell you here and now the biggest threat to the success of business No.1 is your business No. 2.

If your bank balance in one business is not getting increased by €10,000 every single month, you have not yet earned the right to run a second business, and you need to shut one of them down. I don't really care which one you shut down, I don't really care how much you think it doesn't take up any of your time. I'm telling you now 100% your second business is the biggest threat to the success of your first business.

Of the 9 parts of the MAKE-OR-BREAK operating system for your business, this is the part that is regularly overlooked. You might not take it extremely seriously now, but when you have all the other components working as you need them to be working, and you're not getting the result you want, you will revisit this part and you will find you haven't stuck to it correctly.

No second business, no side hustle, no messing around with crypto, forex, stock market, network marketing or whatever else you want to get involved in. All of this stuff has a time and a place and for you, it is only after you begin raising your bank balance by €10k every single month as a result of adopting this operating system that you earn the right to run a second business.

Part 3: Build The Pipeline

The longer and more robust your pipeline is, the stronger your business is. I always recommend aiming for a pipeline of 90 days. I am well aware some businesses will not allow for this length of a pipeline. Anything emergency based is usually not viable for a 90-day pipeline, in which case the business needs to have a complimentary service to allow for this. However, we need to aim for a 90-day pipeline. When building a pipeline, we need to be aware of a practice called segmenting the pipeline.

Here's how it works: let's say you have zero work ahead of you at all. We need to get you some work in the door ASAP. We don't care how much profit is on the work once it's enough to keep the lights on and you can take a wage. This is when the pipeline is 1 day to 30 days in length. This section of the pipeline is called the survival zone, and you must price every job to get it, and you must get every job as if your life depended on it. End of story.

The second section of the pipeline is called the business section, and this is when the pipeline is between 31 days and 60 days in length. You can afford to think like a business owner, and you find that you make €500 in a day the odd time. You price plenty of jobs, you win some and you lose some. You don't mind losing some because you have up to 60 days' work ahead of you. This is the zone where most businesses operate in.

Now we move onto the third section of the pipeline. This is where the magic happens, and we call this the *specialist zone.* When you have 90 days' worth of work ahead of you, you can now price every job with a €500 profit on it. If the job will not give you such profit, you simply refuse to take it on. Now you are a specialist, it is important that you remain as a specialist and stay focused on specialist work that most people will not be willing to do. At this stage, you do not want to be a generalist of any sort. You are the specialist, leave the general work to all the generalists who will fight amongst themselves and undercut each other for the work.

While you remain as a specialist, you will earn like a specialist.

It's super important to be aware of this and not allow yourself to revert back to generalist thinking and do generalist work. That section of your business life is done, and you do not need to go back there.

When you tell people you can't do work for them for up to 90 days down the line and they are telling you they will wait, that's when you know you are in the specialist zone and people now view you as a specialist.

Part 4: Establish The Break-Even Point

Now that you have been made aware of the pipeline and, in particular the segmenting of the pipeline, regardless of what stage of the pipeline you are operating in, you must now establish your BREAK-EVEN point. After all, if you don't know how much money you need to break even, how will you know if you are making a profit or not. This is when it is important to revisit your MAKE-OR- BREAK sheet and see what the figure is that your business needs to make daily to cover all costs, including your wages, your overheads and your €500 a day profit. Don't forget , as we covered in the earlier chapter on the MAKE-OR-BREAK sheet, you have your €500 daily profit included in our break-even point because we are not here to treat our profit as some optional extra we will take at the end if the job allows for it. Our €500 profit is a must have, and that's the end of it. After all, it is part of our mission.

Part 5: The Past Job Analysis

At this point in the proceedings, we are now well aware that we need to be aiming for €500 clear and absolute profit per day. We also know what our daily break-even point is. Now it is time to review your past jobs and see which of these jobs gave you the desired amount of profit and which of these didn't. Obviously, if you are only starting out in business, you won't have this data available to you, and that was the reason we mentioned that it is OK to do work with a low margin on it when we discussed the segmenting of the pipeline.

By allowing yourself to do this lower profit work for 30-60 days, you can collect some data to help you analyse later on.

The past job analysis document can be downloaded from the resources section of my website. This document allows you to review the job and see how much profit was made on the job, versus how much profit was forecast to be made on the job. But here's the magic piece...

The next piece is something that won't be visible to your accountant or be visible in your account's package if looking at the job later on. The PAST JOB ANALYSIS sheet breaks down the profit on the job on a per-day basis.

This means that if you made €4,000 on a job that took you two weeks to complete, and compare this to a job that made you €1,500 in two days, you will see that it's much better for you to spend your time going after the second type of job, as this is where the most profits are available. With this shift in the type of work you allow yourself to go after is super important if you want to become a specialist and you want to hit your €500 profit per day with the least amount of hassle.

Part 6: Build The Campaign

Most of time when chatting with tradesmen, they tell me they are going to up their game and get a website built, and I ask what they are going to put on it and they look a little blank and say just photos of work and what we do and all that. This approach is problematic from the start and here's why.

Your website is purely a brochure to allow people to view your business online. The challenge here is the messaging on the brochure needs to be correct, otherwise it is a waste of time.

Before we go any further, let's just flick back to the start of our MAKE-OR-BREAK operating system one more time and let's see where we are at right now. By now we have:

1. Set the mission for the business.

2. Eliminated all distractions.

3. Built a 90-day pipeline and segmented it.

4. Established our BREAK-EVEN point, which includes €500 daily profit.

5. Carried out a past job analysis on the previous 90 days or more of that work to help us decide what to specialise in.

Now it's time to build the campaign. Let's build the marketing campaign to allow the business to achieve its mission of daily profits of €500 per day by carrying out its most profitable work that it now (or in the very near future) solely specialises in.

Part of the building the campaign entails having your website dedicated solely to the specialist service which it provides. It is not enough in this day and age to merely have a specialist section on your website. You must have your website completely dedicated to the specialist service you provide. If you already have an existing website, leave it there, make a few tweaks but leave it there. Go off and have a specialist website built from scratch. Have all the messaging designed purely to position you as the No.1 for your chosen specialist service in your area. You need to become Mr. Feature Walls, Mr. Wall-Panelling, Mr. Landscaping, Mr. Exterior Painter, Mr. Dry-Dasher. Don't just be a guy who does a bit of this and a bit of that. You need to become the man for this type of work and everything about you should suggest you are the man, from your clothing, your van, your website, your stationery, your attitude.

By the time you have finished this exercise, you should be well on the way to making good money.

Part 7: Insulate As You Go

It is worthwhile reminding you that, in tough times, the businesses with the most cash survive and the way to get yourself in to a position to be able to survive is to insulate yourself with as much cash as possible. What we need to do here is insulate as you go. This means you do not just save vast sums of cash in your business current account. You need to follow a system.

The system we use with my clients from my 52 STEPS mentorship program is we decide how much money we want to make per year from our business. Having a €500 profit per day target will give you a profit of €120k per year but we discount this to €100k for inefficiencies that pop up during the year. This means that 1 x €500 profit per day will give you €100k extra at the end- of-year, 2 x €500 profit per day will give you an extra €200k in the bank at the end of the year.

We break the year up into 7 milestones and at the end of each milestone, there is a transfer date. On the transfer dates, we transfer €14,500 to our savings account.

It's like a mini celebration we get to have 7 times per year. I check in with all of my clients to see how they are getting on, and then they transfer the money across to their savings account and then we simply start again from scratch and get stuck in until the next milestone date which is usually every 7 and a half weeks.

This process is hands down the most effective system for accumulating cash. A typical client when they join my 52 STEPS program will have saved somewhere in the region of up to 45k as a result of all their years in business. After 6 months, they will usually have at least doubled their savings. The reason for this process being so effective is a combination of following all the previous steps plus, by being a part of my mentorship program. We are checking in together every week to make sure they are hitting €500 profit per day as much as possible.

This cash is set aside and taken out of the business current account because we know from experience that if we leave it there, it will get consumed by one thing or other. The other main reason we take the money out of our main current account and put it in to our business savings account, which should not be visible, every time you log in to your online banking, is to avoid the onset of BERTIE BIG BALLS SYNDROME. This is where you start looking at all the money in your account and you start to take your foot off the gas, and you start to get comfortable. Get the money out of your account. Get it set aside and the only reason we spend it is to buy a property, this is called using your business as a vehicle for wealth creation, and it's following this process that has allowed me to build a property portfolio of over €12 million.

If you like this concept and you think you would like to be a part of my 52 STEPS mentorship program, send me an email to jd@joedoyle.ie with the subject 52 STEPS WAITING LIST and we will let you know about our next availability.

Before you begin to set aside money on the regular, you must know how much cash your company needs to hold on to in order to survive and trade on a Day-to-Day basis. We call this amount your ZERO and it's called this because you don't want to allow your bank balance to drop below this. If your ZERO is too high, you will get comfortable, but if your ZERO is too low, it will bring your thinking back into survival mode and we don't want this to be the case. A typical ZERO is usually 6 weeks' running costs, but can vary slightly from business to business.

I have gone through this process with hundreds of clients at this stage, however there are three lads that stand out in my mind, and I feel they deserve a mention here for all of their efforts.

Darragh Carolan of *Crystal Complete Building Services* in North Dublin signed up to do a short one-month program with me about 8 months prior to time of writing. When he signed up, he had no money in his business account. He was literally living out of his overdraft constantly for the previous few years.

Anyway, we got stuck in with him showed him the MAKE-OR-BREAK system and since then he has not missed one milestone payment; he sets aside €14,500 every 7 weeks on our milestone dates and is on track now to have his first 100k by the end of the year.

The one thing that struck me about Darragh was that he never put any obstacles in his own way, and he put 100% faith in me and my system. *"What's next Joe?"*– he would ask and then he would just get on and do it. Not like far too many people who second guess everything and completely stand in their own way the entire time. Darragh my friend, for that I salute you.

Then we have another client of mine, Luke Joyce, from TheCleaningCompany.ie. Luke took to the MAKE-OR-BREAK system like a fish to water. I always try to get lads to look at cash as the key to the next property. If a property deposit is 50k, I look at 25k as half a deposit. I look at 10k as a fifth of a deposit. You know the way certain types of people compare everything to the price of a *'few pints',* we've all heard people say *"sure it was only €150, you would spend that on a night out"*. Well, my benchmark comparison is with the deposit needed to buy a house.

It's a good system in my eyes because when you have 20k saved, you're just about halfway there to the deposit and it keeps you focused and stops you wasting money. Anyway, I was chatting with Luke Joyce on one of our first calls and right away from the outset, he started to link the milestone amounts to the purchase of his first property. He could see that all he had to do was to make €500 in a day and then keep doing this until we got to a certain date in the calendar and a couple of months later he would be in a position to buy a property or have his first €100k in the bank. Just two days before writing this, he sent me a screenshot of his bank account showing he's halfway towards his 100k target in his first year in business. Not bad for a lad who cleans windows and gutters. So Lukey my friend I'm proud of you, just keep doing what you're doing and before long you will have achieved your mission.

Then we have Noel Bolger from Bolger Roofing in Kildare. Noel was flat out doing all sorts of works, but he wasn't hitting the profits that I knew he could hit. Once we got him up to speed on using our system, things started to improve drastically in a short space of time.

'By implementing into my business Joe's MAKE OR BREAK OPERATING SYSTEM it forced me to focus more on the higher value tasks which were critical in order for me to grow my business. I just needed to change my mindset and soon after I started clearing a profit of €500 most days as a two-man operator'. - Noel Bolger

Also, I want to say fair play to the hundreds of other tradesmen who have passed through the doors of my 52 STEPS business mentorship program.

Part 8: Keeping The Score

There is no point in running a business if you don't have a handle on the profits, it's as simple as that. We need to keep track of the numbers, especially the profits, at all times and we need to keep track of them on the daily.

Earlier on in chapter 6, we looked in detail at the MAKE-OR-BREAK Sheet. The MAKE-OR-BREAK sheet is one of the tools that forms a central part of the MAKE-OR-BREAK BUSINESS OPERATING SYSTEM. It's now time to revisit this part again. It is essential that you now get your MAKE-OR-BREAK Board and hang it on the wall in your office if you haven't already done so.

This board needs to be completed every single day. It only takes a few minutes to complete, and every day you say you don't have time to complete it, you need to remember that it's not a lack of time that is holding you back from completing it; it's actually a lack of discipline. If you want to succeed at getting the most out of your business, and if you want to succeed in implementing the MAKE-OR-BREAK BUSINESS OPERATING SYSTEM, you need to make sure you develop the discipline required in order to complete the MAKE-OR- BREAK board on a daily basis.

By completing the MAKE-OR-BREAK board on a daily basis, you will know at the end of every single day how much profit your company has made. To set up the MAKE-OR-BREAK board correctly, it requires a little bit of effort and a bit of getting used to.

To help with this, we have provided a tutorial video in the resources that accompany this book, so be sure to check that out.

As I say, you would not have 7 showers on a Sunday to make up for the lack of washing all week, so you need to take the same approach with the MAKE-OR-BREAK Board. From all the couple of thousand tradesmen who have passed through my business mentorship program, the ones who get the best results are the ones who actually develop the discipline to complete the Make-Or-Break Board on a daily basis.

Part 9: Community & Accountability

Each item in the MAKE-OR-BREAK OPERATING SYSTEM is fundamentally important to the success of the business. However, the final part, being the community part, multiplies the effectiveness of each part of the entire process. If you find yourself involved with a community of lads who are all in top physical shape due to them playing sports or going to the gym every day after work, I can pretty much guarantee you that before long, you will start to become more '*fitness aware*' yourself, and you will start to make advances in that direction. The exact same can be said if you find yourself in a community of people who like to head for pints all the time after work, or who want to head out on the lash for every possible reason. If you hang out with these people all the time, chances are soon enough you will start to make moves in this direction yourself.

When it comes to your business, it's the same. As we all know, running a business can be a lonely place at times. When things are going wrong, the only people usually who we can speak to, that we trust, are our family members, and let's be honest, unless they have a business themselves, they won't understand you. You can, of course, chat to your staff, your suppliers, your contractors or your competitors. Some of these guys will understand where you are coming from, but they are the last people who you want to be sharing your business thoughts, plans and concerns with.

This is why community and accountability is so important for business. I have been running my business community, which is part of my 52 STEPS to a better business program, for 5 years at the time of writing. Every week we check in with the lads to see who has hit their €500 profit every day and who has not hit it, and more importantly, why they have not hit it.

Every week we get lads who have not sent in their accountability email, and that's fine. But the thing is, they are usually still tuned in to the session, and these guys know that in order for them to stay performing at the new higher level they are currently performing at, they need to be checking in and following each step of the process. From time to time lads drop off for a few weeks here or there, and then they come back to me and tell me that productivity started to drop, and they started going back to their old ways, and it was only the regular check-ins with the community of lads in the group that helped them regain their focus and get back on track.

You know the old saying: *"If you hang around the barber shop long enough, it won't be long before you get yourself a haircut."* The same goes for following the MAKE-OR-BREAK OPERATING SYSTEM and more importantly, if you hang around in my 52 STEPS community for any length of time, you're going to end up making more money, simple as that.

Final Thoughts

You might be asking yourself, *"If this is so good, why is he telling us for free?"*, or *"Why isn't he using it himself?"*; so let me break that down for you into two answers.

I am happy to tell you how to do this for free but if you want me personally to help you implement it, you will have to hire me, it's a simple enough philosophy in my opinion.

"Why isn't he using it himself?", the truth is I most definitely am using this system myself. I believe my system is transferable to any business, and I used it in my own construction business for 10 years before I got out of the game to focus on building my property portfolio (If you don't

know much about what I have achieved so far, I will let you do a little Google search to find out for yourself).

The fact that it worked for me in the building game means that when I chat with someone else in the building game and they tell me it won't work, I know it is down to them not applying it correctly. Maybe over time I will promote the MAKE OR BREAK OPERATING SYSTEM to others, but for now I think I've got enough to do implementing it with the building industry.

In all my years of business I have never felt so confident of the commitment and ability of all my team. I would like to say a special thanks to all my team and clients.

In particular I want to say thanks to

Paddy

Karl

Alan

Jaybear

Cameron

Darren

&

Jean

Thank you for all the help with bringing the book to fruition.